# Standard Grade | General | Credit

# Geography

General Level 1999
General Level 2000
General Level 2001
General Level 2002
General Level 2003
Credit Level 1999
Credit Level 2000
Credit Level 2001
Credit Level 2002
Credit Level 2003

First exam published in 1999.
Published by
Leckie & Leckie, 8 Whitehill Terrace, St. Andrews, Scotland KY16 8RN
tel: 01334 475656  fax: 01334 477392
enquiries@leckieandleckie.co.uk www.leckieandleckie.co.uk

Leckie & Leckie Project Team: Peter Dennis; John MacPherson; Bruce Ryan; Andrea Smith

ISBN 1-84372-095-7

A CIP Catalogue record for this book is available from the British Library.

Printed in Scotland by Scotprint.

Leckie & Leckie is a division of Granada Learning Limited, part of Granada plc.

Leckie ×Leckie
Scotland's leading educational publishers

# Introduction

Dear Student,

This past paper book offers you the perfect opportunity to put into practice what you should know in order to do well in your exams. As these questions have actually appeared in the exam in previous years, you can be sure they reflect the kind of questions you will be asked this summer.

Work carefully through the papers, not only to test your knowledge and understanding but also your ability to handle information and work through more thought-provoking questions. Use the answer booklet at the back of the book to check that you know exactly what the examiner is looking for to gain top marks. You will be able to focus on areas of weakness to sharpen your grasp of the subject and our top tips for revision and sitting the exam will also help to improve your performance on the day.

Remember, practice makes perfect! These past papers will show you what to expect in your exam, help to boost your confidence and feel ready to gain the grade you really want.

Good luck!

# Acknowledgements

Leckie & Leckie is grateful to the copyright holders, as credited, for permission to use their material. Every effort has been made to trace the copyright holders and to obtain their permission for the use of copyright material. Leckie & Leckie will gladly receive information enabling them to rectify any error or omission in subsequent editions.

The maps have been reproduced by kind permission of Ordnance Survey. © Crown Copyright NC/02/28038.

G

| KU | ES |
|---|---|
| | |

Total Marks

# 1260/103

SCOTTISH
CERTIFICATE OF
EDUCATION
1999

TUESDAY, 11 MAY
G/C   9.00 AM – 10.25 AM
F/G  10.25 AM – 11.50 AM

## GEOGRAPHY
## STANDARD GRADE
General Level

---

**Fill in these boxes and read what is printed below.**

Full name of school or college

Town

First name and initials

Surname

Date of birth
Day  Month  Year        Candidate number        Number of seat

1  Read the whole of each question carefully before you answer it.

2  Write in the spaces provided.

3  Where boxes like this ☐ are provided, put a tick ✓ in the box beside the answer you think is correct.

4  Try all the questions.

5  Do not give up the first time you get stuck:  you may be able to answer later questions.

6  Extra paper may be obtained from the invigilator, if required.

7  Before leaving the examination room you must give this book to the invigilator.  If you do not, you may lose all the marks for this paper.

SCOTTISH
QUALIFICATIONS
AUTHORITY

Extract No 1137/66

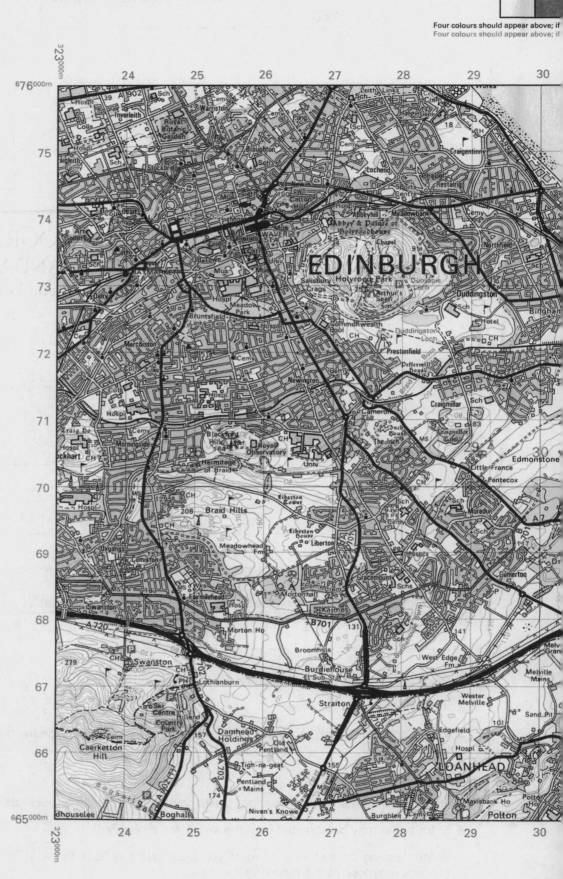

Magnetic North  Grid North  True North

Diagrammatic
only

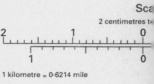

Sca

2 centimetres te

2     1     0

1     0

1 kilometre = 0·6214 mile

**1:50 000 Scale
Landranger Series**

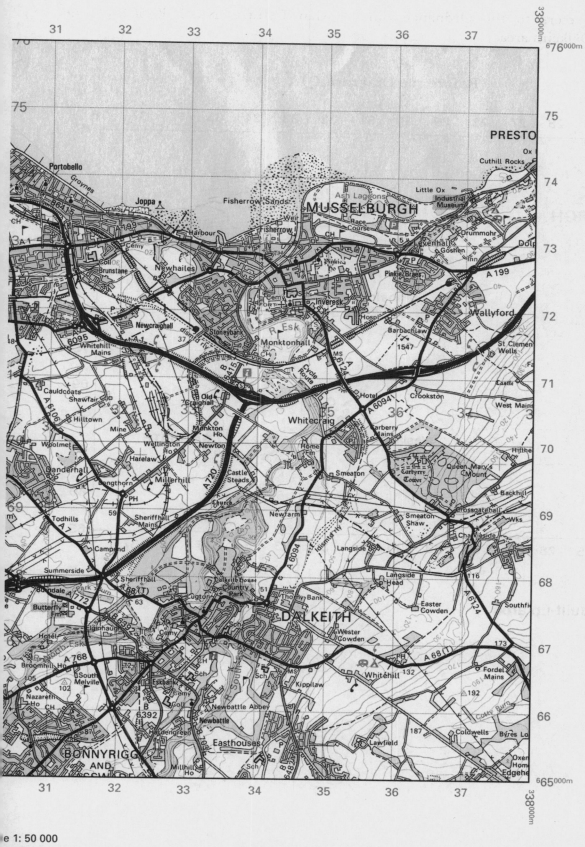

1. Question 1 refers to the Ordnance Survey Map Extract (No 1137/66) of the Edinburgh/Dalkeith area.

### Reference Diagram Q1A

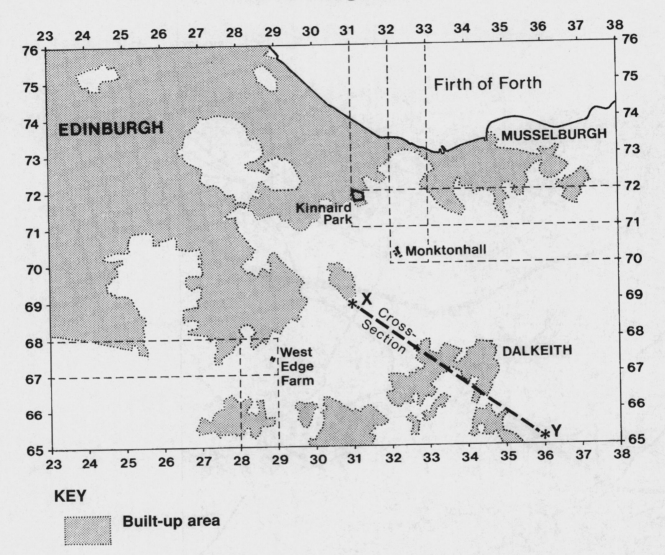

KEY

▦ Built-up area

**1. (continued)**

**Reference Diagram Q1B: Cross-section XY from 310689 to 360652**

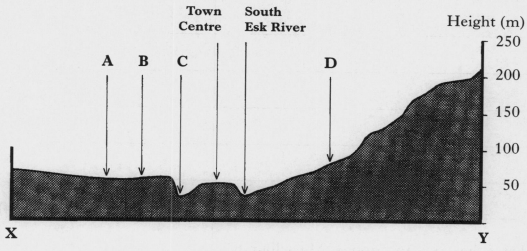

Horizontal scale ⌐ 1 km ⌐

(a)  Look at Reference Diagram Q1B.

Match the Features (**A**, **B**, **C** and **D**) on the cross-section **XY** with the correct descriptions in the table below.

| Feature | Letter |
|---|---|
| Woodland | |
| North Esk River | |
| A 720 | |
| B 6482 | |

(3)

(b)  Using **specific** examples from the map, **describe** the ways in which Dalkeith's growth has been restricted.

_____

_____

_____

_____

_____

_____

(4)

KU | ES

*Marks*

**1. (continued)**

(c) Kinnaird Park, a shopping and leisure complex, was built at 312718.

Using map evidence, **explain** why this location was chosen.

_____

_____

_____

_____

_____

_____

**(4)**

(d) What is the main **function** of Musselburgh?

Tick (✓) your choice.

Holiday Resort ☐          Commuter Settlement ☐

Use map evidence to support your choice.

_____

_____

_____

_____

_____

**(4)**

KU | ES

KU | ES

Marks

**1. (continued)**

(e) Match the following grid squares with the land uses shown in the table below.

Grid squares: 2573    2671    2372    2868

| Land Use | Grid Square |
|---|---|
| Mixture of old housing and old industry | |
| Central Business District (CBD) | |
| Modern housing area | |
| Older housing area | |

**(3)**

(f) West Edge Farm is located at 289674. Do you think this is a good location for a farm?

Tick (✓) your choice.    YES ☐    NO ☐

**Using map evidence**, give reasons to support your choice.

_____

_____

_____

_____

_____

_____

**(4)**

**[Turn over**

KU | ES

*Marks*

## 1. (continued)

### Reference Diagram Q1C: Demolition of Mining Towers at Monktonhall

(g)  Look at Reference Diagram Q1C.

The coal mine at 3270 was closed in June 1997.

Give the advantages **and** disadvantages of the closure of the mine **to** the surrounding area.

(You should refer to the sketch and/or map evidence to support your answer.)

Advantages _____

_____

_____

_____

Disadvantages _____

_____

_____

_____

_____

**(4)**

2.    **Reference Diagram Q2:  Weather Chart for 1200 hours
on 25 November**

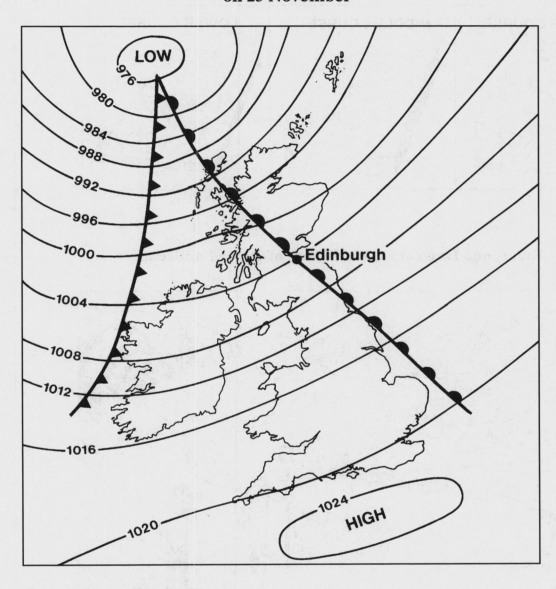

Look at Reference Diagram Q2.

**Describe** the weather conditions in Edinburgh at 1200 hours on 25 November.

_____

_____

_____

_____

_____

_____    (4)

**3.**  **Reference Diagram Q3A:  Three Stages of a River**

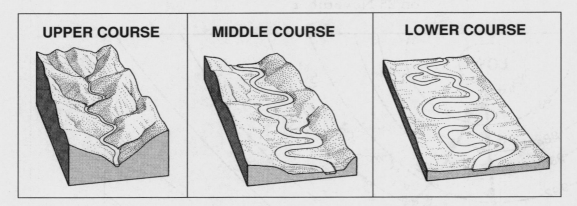

**Reference Diagram Q3B:  Sketch of River Landscape**

Marks

KU ES

**3. (continued)**

(a)   Look at Reference Diagrams Q3A and Q3B.

"The valley shown in Reference Diagram Q3B is typical of the **lower** course of a river."

Do you agree with the statement?

Tick (✓) your choice.     YES ☐     NO ☐

Give reasons for your choice.

_____

_____

_____

_____

_____

**(4)**

(b)   The pupils in Reference Diagram Q3B are about to do a river study.

What **two** techniques could they use to gather information about the characteristics of the river at **AB** on the sketch?

Technique 1  _____

_____

Technique 2  _____

_____

Justify your choices.

_____

_____

_____

_____

**(4)**

**[Turn over**

4.   **Reference Diagram Q4A:  Climate Graph of Tropical Rainforest**

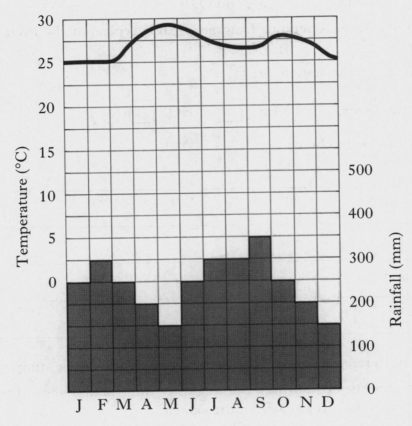

**Reference Diagram Q4B:  Developing the Tropical Rainforest**

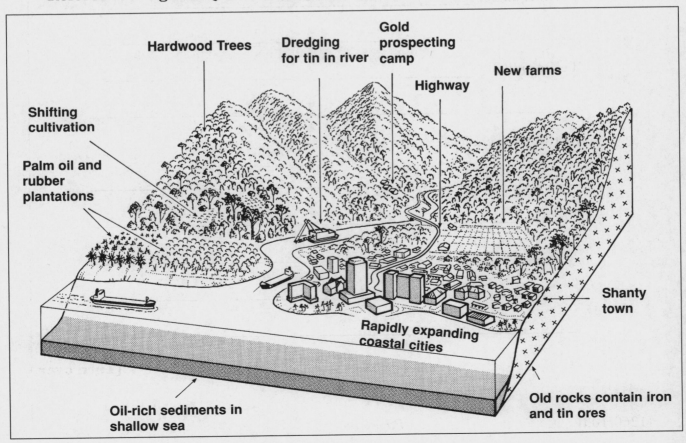

| | KU | ES |
|---|---|---|

*Marks*

**4. (continued)**

(*a*)    Look at Reference Diagram Q4A.

     **Describe** in detail the climate of the Tropical Rainforest.

_____

_____

_____

_____

_____

**(3)**

(*b*)    Look at Reference Diagram Q4B.

     **Describe** the damage to the environment which could be caused by developing the natural resources of a Tropical Rainforest.

_____

_____

_____

_____

_____

**(4)**

**[Turn over**

KU | ES

*Marks*

**5.**  **Reference Diagram Q5:  Farming Landscape**

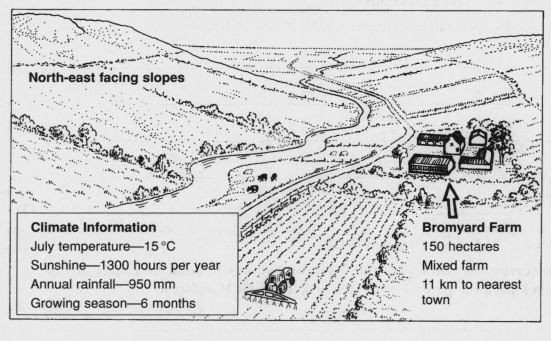

**North-east facing slopes**

**Climate Information**
July temperature—15 °C
Sunshine—1300 hours per year
Annual rainfall—950 mm
Growing season—6 months

**Bromyard Farm**
150 hectares
Mixed farm
11 km to nearest
town

Look at Reference Diagram Q5.

"Mixed Farming is the most suitable type of farming for this area."

Do you agree with the statement?

Tick (✓) your choice.      YES  ☐      NO  ☐

Give detailed reasons for your choice.

_____

_____

_____

_____

_____

_____

**(4)**

**6.**  **Reference Diagram Q6: The M62 Corridor**

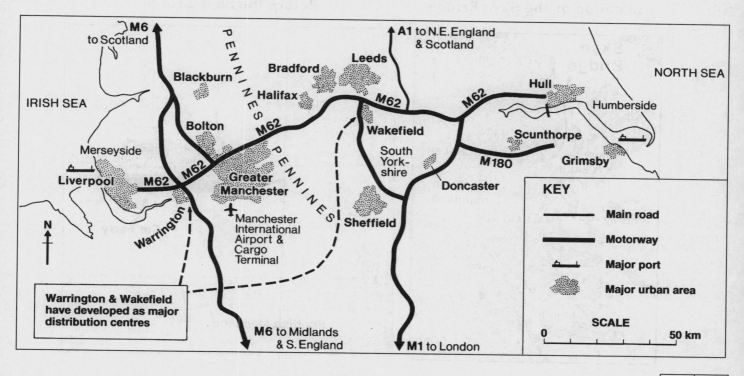

Look at Reference Diagram Q6.

The M62 motorway runs from Merseyside to Humberside. The area around it, known as the M62 corridor, is often described as England's new economic super region.

Give reasons to **explain** why so many companies are locating here.

Marks

(4)

[Turn over

**7.** **Reference Diagram Q7A:**
**Location of the Skye Bridge**

**Reference Diagram Q7B:**
**Before the Skye Bridge**

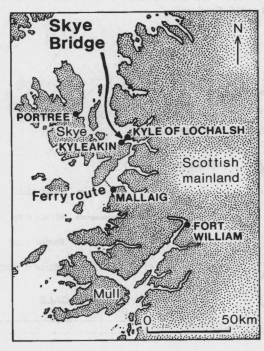

**Reference Diagram Q7C: The Skye Bridge**

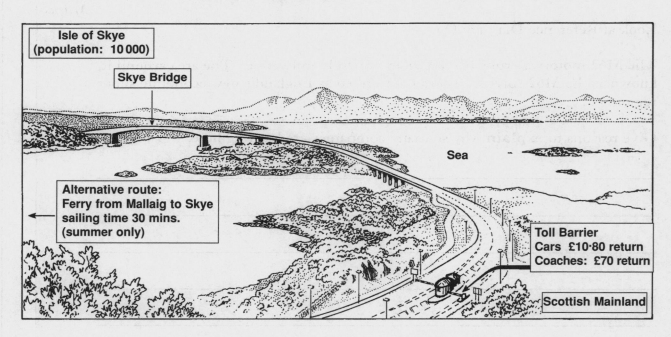

Isle of Skye
(population: 10 000)

Skye Bridge

Sea

Alternative route:
Ferry from Mallaig to Skye
sailing time 30 mins.
(summer only)

Toll Barrier
Cars £10·80 return
Coaches: £70 return

Scottish Mainland

KU | ES

*Marks*

## 7. (continued)

Look at Reference Diagrams Q7A, Q7B and Q7C.

The Skye Bridge was opened in 1996 and replaced the ferry which ran from Kyle of Lochalsh to Kyleakin.

Give advantages **and** disadvantages of the Skye Bridge **for the people of Skye**.

Advantages _____

_____

_____

_____

_____

Disadvantages _____

_____

_____

_____

**(4)**

**[Turn over**

**8.**    **Reference Diagram Q8A:  Japan's Trade Links**

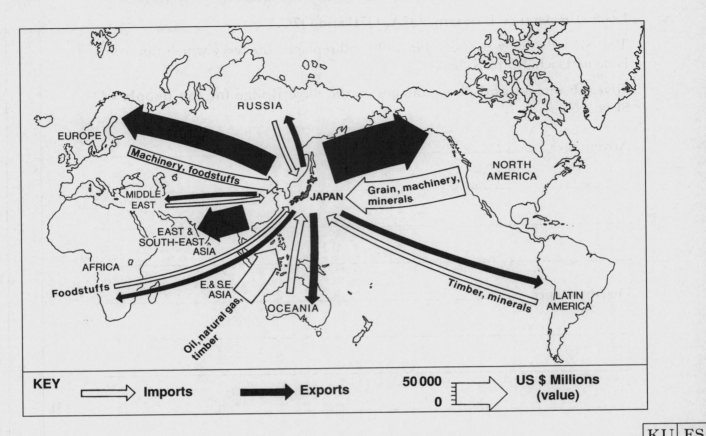

KEY    ⇨ **Imports**    ⬛➤ **Exports**    50 000 / 0    **US $ Millions (value)**

|  | KU | ES |
|---|---|---|

*Marks*

(a)    Look at Reference Diagram Q8A.

**Describe** the pattern of Japan's trade.

_____

_____

_____

_____

_____

_____

**(3)**

KU | ES

*Marks*

**8. (continued)**

**Reference Diagram Q8B: Japan's Exports**

| Exports | Percentage |
|---|---|
| Manufactured goods | 83 |
| Chemicals and other raw materials | 7 |
| Others | 10 |

(b)  Look at Reference Diagram Q8B.

Give **one** processing technique which could be used to present the information in Reference Diagram Q8B.  Give reasons for your choice.

Technique  _____

Reasons  _____

_____

_____

_____

_____

_____

**(3)**

**[Turn over**

9. **Reference Diagram Q9: Distribution of Underweight Children**

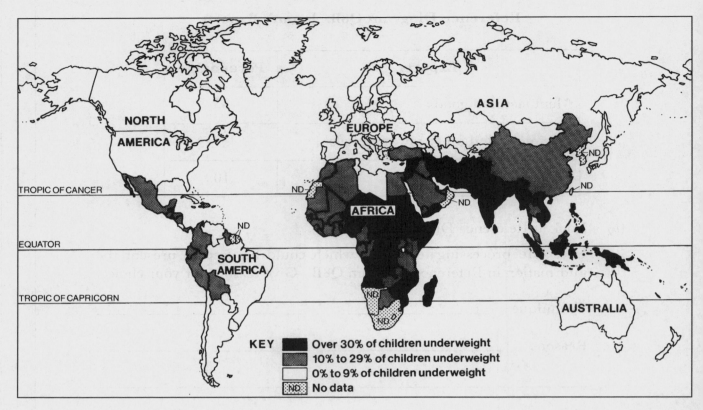

KEY
- Over 30% of children underweight
- 10% to 29% of children underweight
- 0% to 9% of children underweight
- ND No data

|  | KU | ES |
|---|---|---|
| *Marks* | | |

Look at Reference Diagram Q9.

(*a*) **Describe** the distribution pattern of underweight children.

_____

_____

_____

_____

_____

_____    **(3)**

Marks

KU | ES

**9. (continued)**

*(b)* **Explain** why certain parts of the world have a high percentage of underweight children.

_____

_____

_____

_____

_____

_____ **(4)**

**[Turn over for Question 10 on *Page twenty***

KU | ES

*Marks*

10.  **Reference Diagram Q10:  Maps of Malaysian Peninsula**

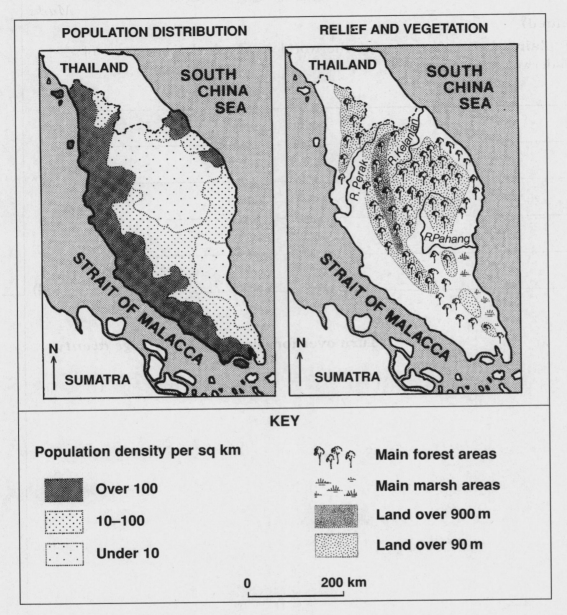

POPULATION DISTRIBUTION

RELIEF AND VEGETATION

**KEY**

**Population density per sq km**

Over 100

10–100

Under 10

Main forest areas

Main marsh areas

Land over 900 m

Land over 90 m

0        200 km

Look at Reference Diagram Q10 above.

**Describe** the relationship between population distribution and physical features (relief and vegetation) in the Malaysian Peninsula.

_____

_____

_____

_____

_____

_____

**(4)**

*[END OF QUESTION PAPER]*

FOR OFFICIAL USE

**G**

KU    ES

Total Marks

**1260/403**

NATIONAL
QUALIFICATIONS
2000

MONDAY, 5 JUNE
G/C   9.00 AM – 10.25 AM
F/G   10.25 AM – 11.50 AM

**GEOGRAPHY
STANDARD GRADE**
General Level

---

**Fill in these boxes and read what is printed below.**

Full name of centre

Town

Forename(s)

Surname

Date of birth
Day  Month  Year       Scottish candidate number       Number of seat

1  Read the whole of each question carefully before you answer it.

2  Write in the spaces provided.

3  Where boxes like this ☐ are provided, put a tick ✓ in the box beside the answer you think is correct.

4  Try all the questions.

5  Do not give up the first time you get stuck:  you may be able to answer later questions.

6  Extra paper may be obtained from the invigilator, if required.

7  Before leaving the examination room you must give this book to the invigilator.  If you do not, you may lose all the marks for this paper.

SCOTTISH
QUALIFICATIONS
AUTHORITY

©

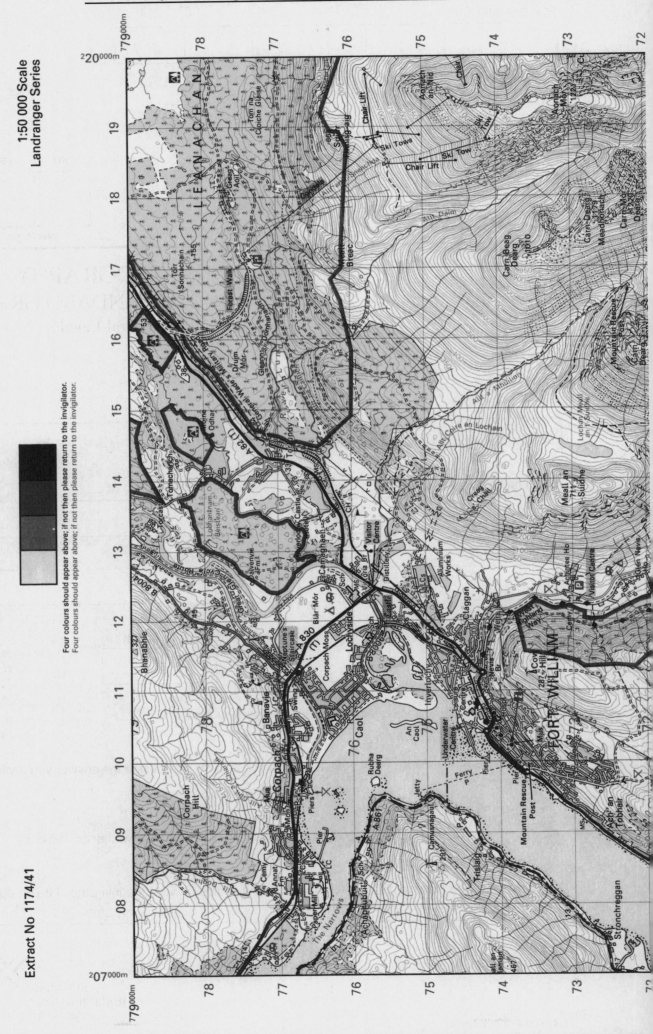

Extract No 1174/41

1:50 000 Scale
Landranger Series

Four colours should appear above; if not then please return to the invigilator.
Four colours should appear above; if not then please return to the invigilator.

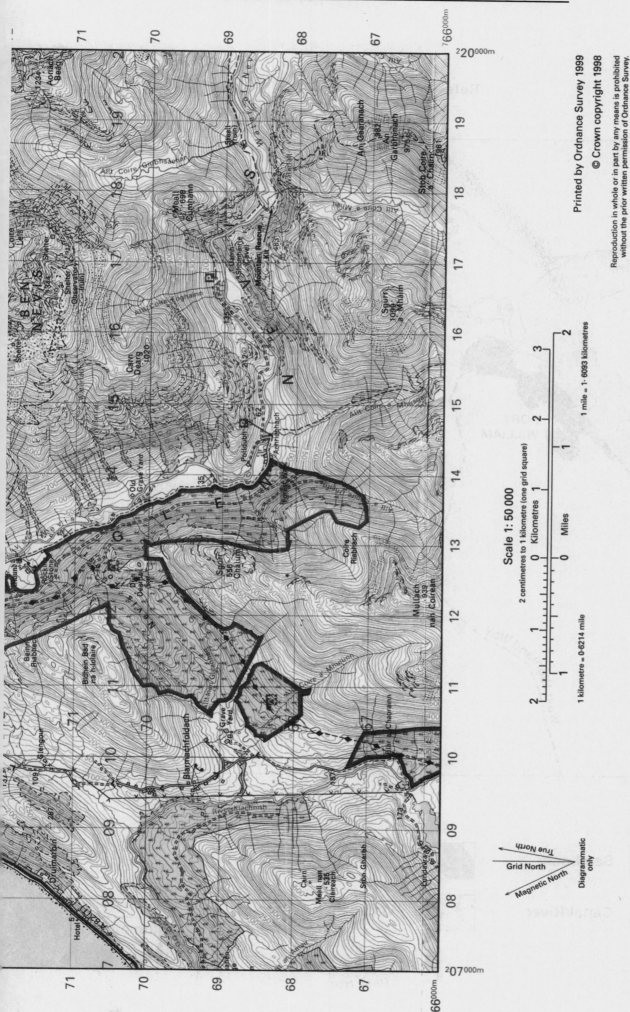

Scale 1: 50 000

2 centimetres to 1 kilometre (one grid square)

1 kilometre = 0·6214 mile

1 mile = 1· 6093 kilometres

Printed by Ordnance Survey 1999

© Crown copyright 1998

Reproduction in whole or in part by any means is prohibited
without the prior written permission of Ordnance Survey.

Map reproduced from Ordnance Survey mapping with the permission of the
Controller of Her Majesty's Stationery Office, © Crown copyright, Licence No. 100036009.

**1.**                    **Reference Diagram Q1A**

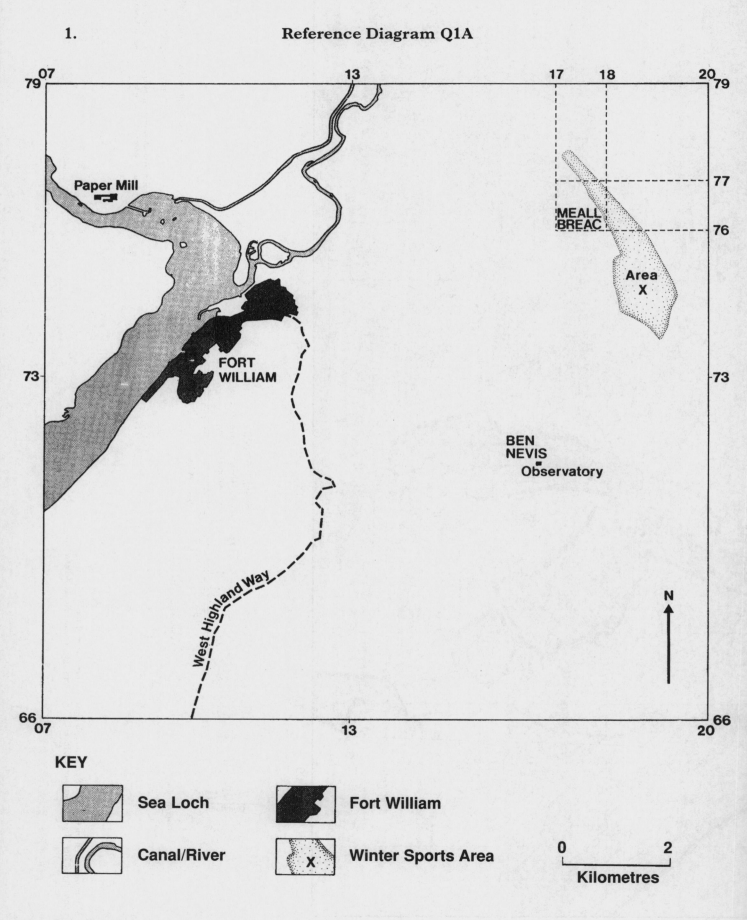

**KEY**

Sea Loch

Canal/River

Fort William

X  Winter Sports Area

0          2
**Kilometres**

*Marks*

## 1. (continued)

Look at the Ordnance Survey Map Extract (No 1174/41) of the Fort William area and Reference Diagram Q1A on *Page two*.

(a)  Using map evidence, describe the advantages **and** disadvantages of the site of Fort William.

Advantages _____

_____

_____

_____

Disadvantages _____

_____

_____

_____

4

(b)  Area X on Reference Diagram Q1A has been developed for skiing.

**Using map evidence**, **describe** the likely effects this has had on the area covered by the whole map extract.

_____

_____

_____

_____

_____

_____

_____

4

**[Turn over**

*Marks*

## 1. (continued)

### Reference Diagram Q1B: An Aerial View looking south from above Meall Breac (1776)

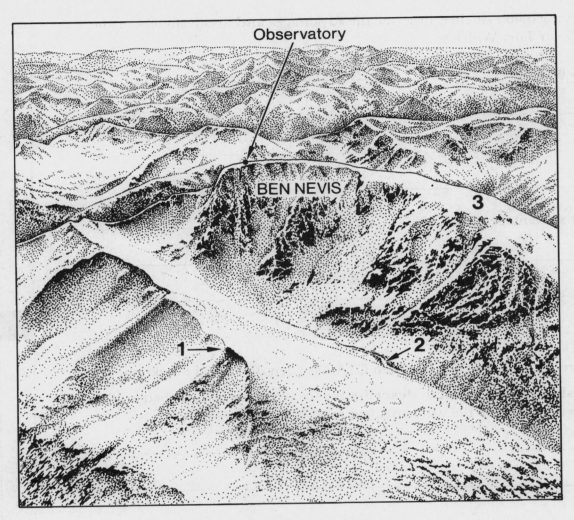

(c)  Look at Reference Diagram Q1A, Reference Diagram Q1B and the map extract.

Identify the three features marked 1, 2 and 3.

Choose from:

Allt a Mhuilinn, Sgurr a Mhaim, Carn Beag Dearg, Carn Dearg.

1 _____

2 _____

3 _____   **3**

*Marks*

## 1. (continued)

(d)   Match each of the glacial features in the table below to the correct grid square.

Grid squares:   1869      1674      1272      1771

| Glacial Features | Grid Square |
|---|---|
| Arête | |
| Hanging Valley | |
| "U" Shaped Valley | |

3

(e)   **Explain** how **one** of the glacial features listed in (d) was formed.  You may use a sketch to illustrate your answer.

_____

_____

_____

_____

_____

_____

_____

_____

_____

_____

3

**[Turn over**

*Marks*

### 1. (continued)

(*f*) There is a large paper mill in grid square 0876.

**Explain** why this site is a suitable location for the paper mill. You **must** use map evidence.

_____

_____

_____

_____

_____

_____

4

*Marks*

## 1. (continued)

**Reference Diagram Q1C:  Erosion along the West Highland Way**

(g)  Look at Reference Diagram Q1C above and the statement given below.

"Footpath erosion along the West Highland Way is now spoiling a beautiful landscape."

Give **two** gathering techniques which could be used when carrying out a study of footpath erosion.

Why are these techniques suitable?

_____

_____

_____

_____

_____

_____

_____

_____

4

*Marks*

2.   **Reference Diagram Q2:  Weather Conditions in Scotland
November 1995**

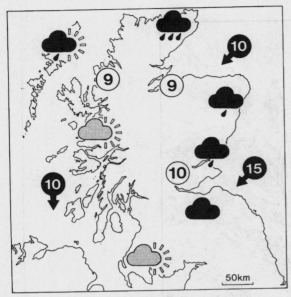

**FRIDAY 9 NOVEMBER**

**SATURDAY 10 NOVEMBER**

**Key to Symbols**

Look at Reference Diagram Q2.

**Compare** Friday's weather with Saturday's weather along the **east** coast of
Scotland.  You must refer to **more than one** weather element.

_____

_____

_____

_____

_____

_____

_____

_____

4

*Marks*

3. **Reference Diagram Q3: Land Uses in the Countryside**

Look at Reference Diagram Q3.

"There are possible conflicts between the land uses shown."

Do you agree with the above statement?

Tick (✓) the box.　　YES ☐　　NO ☐

**Explain** your answer.

_____

_____

_____

_____

_____

_____

_____

4

Marks

4.  **Reference Diagram Q4:  Climate Graph for Athens (Greece)**

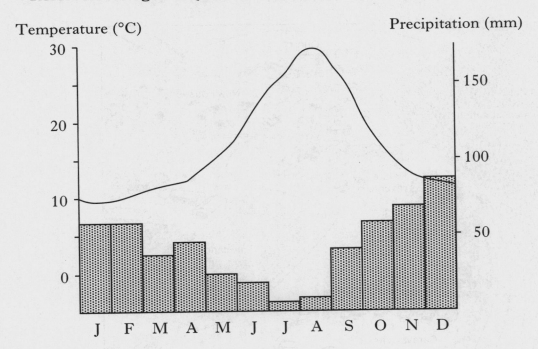

(a)  **Describe** in detail the climate shown in Reference Diagram Q4.

_____

_____

_____

_____

3

(b)  What are the likely advantages **and** disadvantages of the climate shown
in Reference Diagram Q4 for **people** living in areas which have this type
of climate?

Advantages  _____

_____

_____

_____

Disadvantages  _____

_____

_____

_____

4

*Marks*

**5.**　　　　**Reference Diagram Q5:　Greater Manchester**

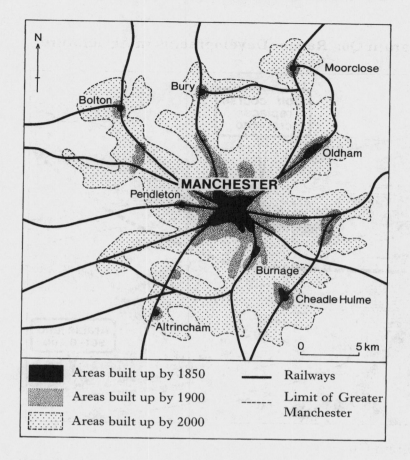

Areas built up by 1850
Areas built up by 1900
Areas built up by 2000

Railways
Limit of Greater
Manchester

0　　　　5 km

Look at Reference Diagram Q5.

(*a*)　**Describe** the way Manchester has grown since 1850.

_____

_____

_____

_____

_____

**3**

(*b*)　**Describe** the methods used to limit the growth of large urban areas such as Greater Manchester.

_____

_____

_____

_____

_____

**4**

[1260/403]　　　　　　　　　*Page eleven*　　　　　　　　　**[Turn over**

*Marks*

6.    **Reference Diagram Q6:  Recent Developments in Agriculture**

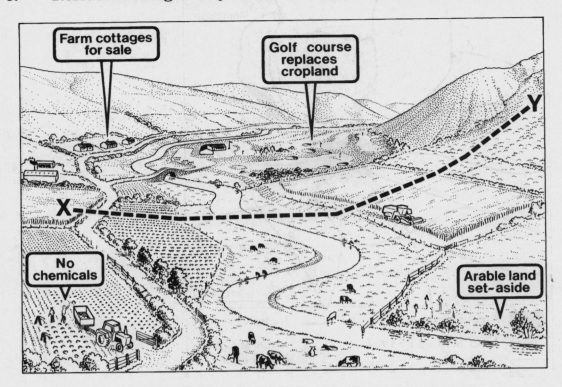

Look at Reference Diagram Q6.

(a)  Choose **two** of the developments in agriculture shown in the above diagram and give reasons why each one is taking place.

Development _____

Explanation _____

_____

_____

_____

_____

Development _____

Explanation _____

_____

_____

_____

_____

4

KU | ES

*Marks*

6. **(continued)**

(b)   Information has been gathered along line **X–Y** on land use and height. What technique would you use to show this information?

Give reasons for your choice of technique.

_____

_____

_____

_____

_____

_____

**3**

**[Turn over**

KU | ES

**7.** **Reference Diagram Q7: Developing World Migration Model**

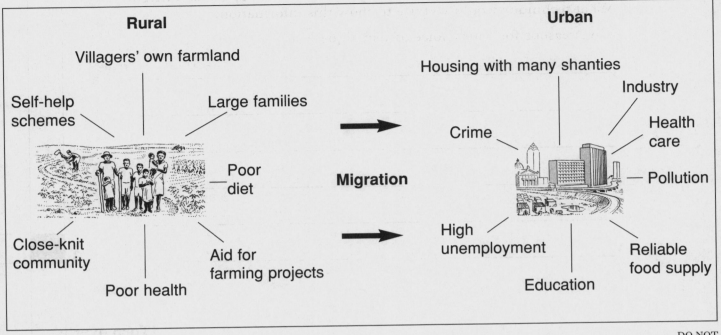

DO NOT WRITE IN THIS MARGIN

| KU | ES |
|----|----|

*Marks*

"Migration is always a move to better opportunities."

Do you agree with the statement?

Tick (✓) your choice.     YES ☐     NO ☐

Give reasons for your choice.

_____

_____

_____

_____

_____

_____

_____

4

*Marks*

**8.** (*a*) A population pyramid for France is drawn below (Reference Diagram Q8A).

**Reference Diagram Q8A**

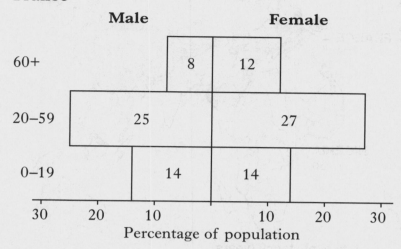

France

**Reference Table Q8B:  Age Structure of Population**

|  | Age Groups | Male % of population | Female % of population |
|---|---|---|---|
| **Nigeria** | 60+ | 3 | 3 |
| | 20–59 | 19 | 18 |
| | 0–19 | 28 | 29 |

**Reference Diagram Q8C**

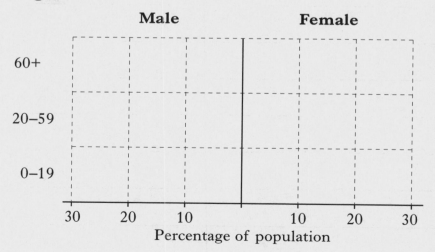

Nigeria

Use the information in Reference Table Q8B to complete the population pyramid for Nigeria (Reference Diagram Q8C).

**3**

*Marks*

**8. (continued)**

### Reference Diagram Q8D: Life Expectancy

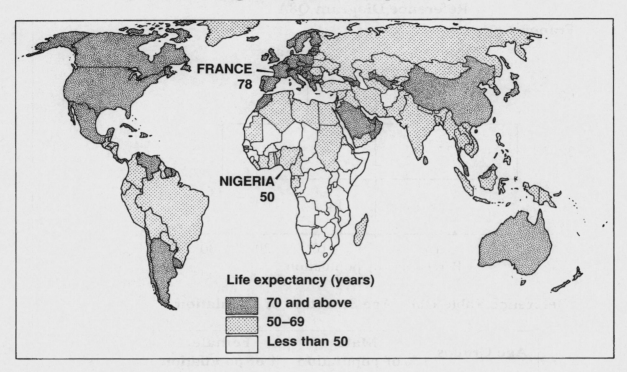

FRANCE
78

NIGERIA
50

**Life expectancy (years)**

70 and above
50–69
Less than 50

(*b*)    Look at Reference Diagram Q8D above.

**Explain** why Life Expectancy is higher in France than in Nigeria.

_____

_____

_____

_____

_____

_____

_____

_____

_____

4

DO NOT
WRITE IN
THIS
MARGIN

KU ES

*Marks*

9. **Reference Diagram Q9: Hurricane Disaster in Central America**

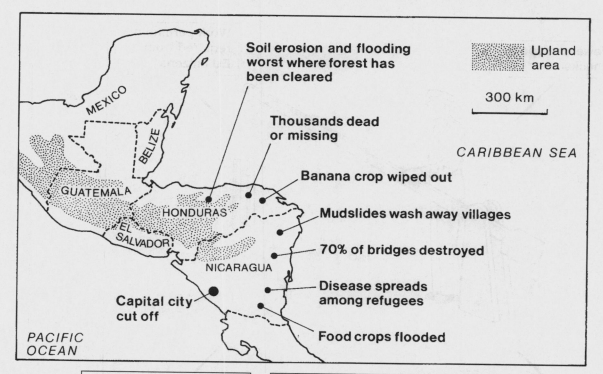

| Short Term Aid | Long Term Aid |
|---|---|
| • deals with the most urgent problems | • aid which rebuilds and develops a country over several years |

Look at Reference Diagram Q9.

"Only short term aid can help Central America recover from Hurricane
Mitch." (UN Spokesperson 1998)

Do you agree with the statement?

Tick (✓) your choice.     YES [ ]     NO [ ]

Give reasons for your choice.

Reasons _____

_____

_____

_____

_____

_____

_____

4

KU | ES

*Marks*

**10.**     **Reference Diagram Q10: Europe's Open Borders**

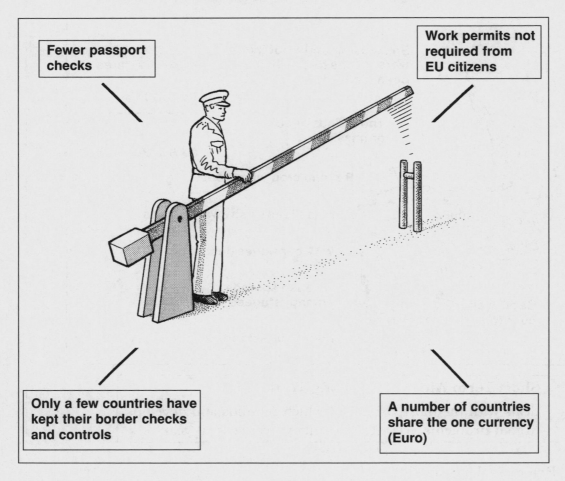

**Fewer passport checks**

**Work permits not required from EU citizens**

**Only a few countries have kept their border checks and controls**

**A number of countries share the one currency (Euro)**

Look at Reference Diagram Q10 which shows new arrangements for EU member countries.

**Explain** the advantages of the new arrangements to the people living in the European Union.

_____

_____

_____

_____

_____

4

[*END OF QUESTION PAPER*]

FOR OFFICIAL USE

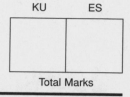

KU | ES

**Total Marks**

## 1260/403

NATIONAL
QUALIFICATIONS
2001

WEDNESDAY, 23 MAY
G/C   9.00 AM – 10.25 AM
F/G   10.25 AM – 11.50 AM

**GEOGRAPHY**
**STANDARD GRADE**
General Level

**Fill in these boxes and read what is printed below.**

Full name of centre

Town

Forename(s)

Surname

Date of birth
Day  Month  Year      Scottish candidate number      Number of seat

1  Read the whole of each question carefully before you answer it.

2  Write in the spaces provided.

3  Where boxes like this ☐ are provided, put a tick ✓ in the box beside the answer you think is correct.

4  Try all the questions.

5  Do not give up the first time you get stuck:  you may be able to answer later questions.

6  Extra paper may be obtained from the invigilator, if required.

7  Before leaving the examination room you must give this book to the invigilator.  If you do not, you may lose all the marks for this paper.

SCOTTISH
QUALIFICATIONS
AUTHORITY

©

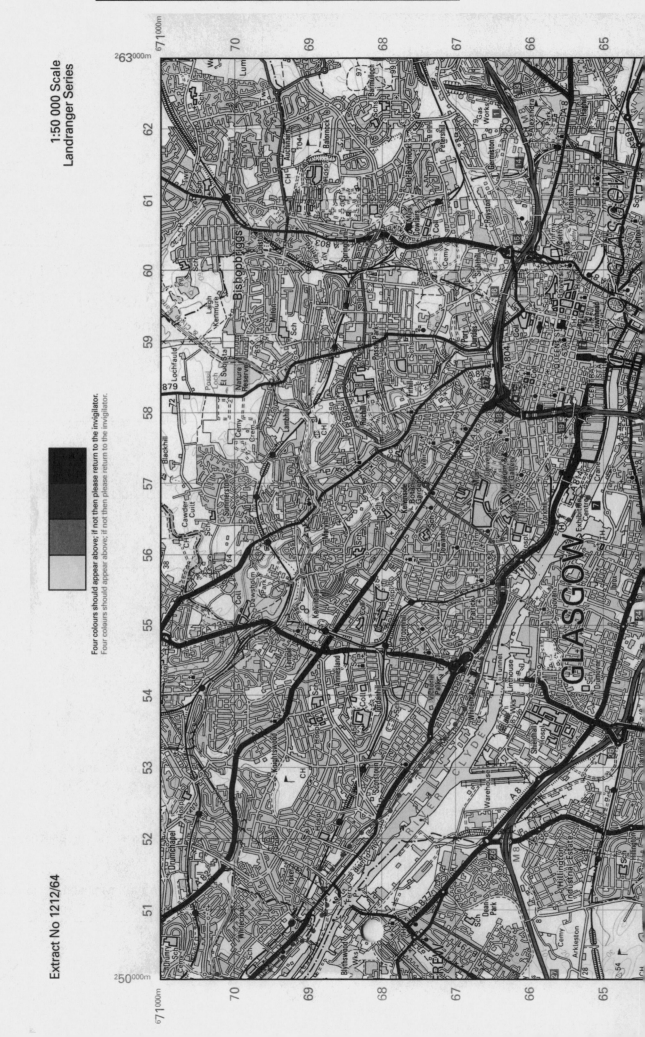

1:50 000 Scale
Landranger Series

Four colours should appear above; if not then please return to the invigilator.
Four colours should appear above; if not then please return to the invigilator.

Extract No 1212/64

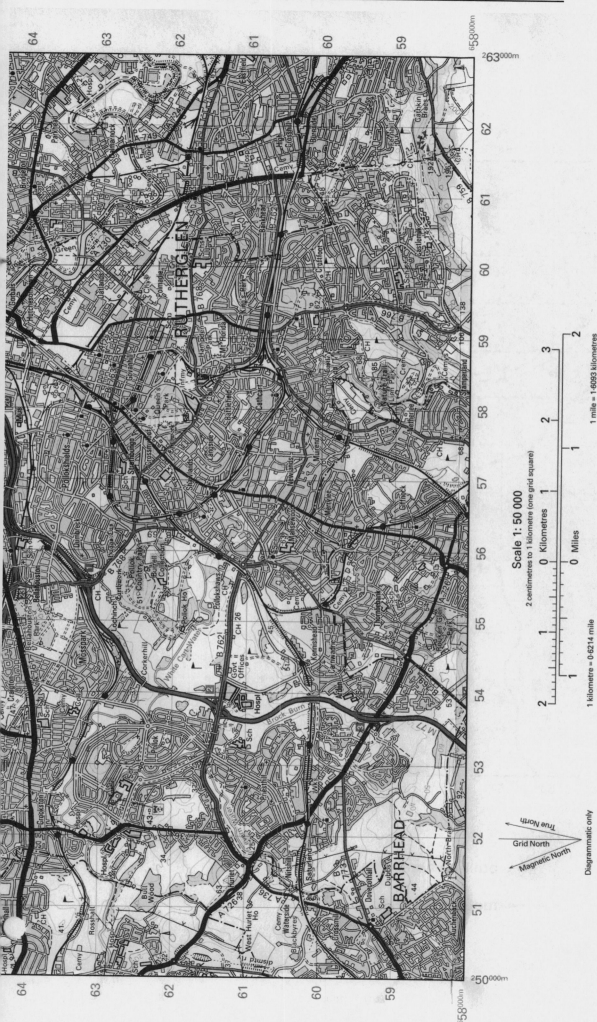

Scale 1: 50 000

2 centimetres to 1 kilometre (one grid square)

1 mile = 1·6093 kilometres

1 kilometre = 0·6214 mile

Grid North
True North
Magnetic North

Diagrammatic only

Map reproduced from Ordnance Survey mapping with the permission of the
Controller of Her Majesty's Stationery Office, © Crown copyright, Licence No. 100036009.

**1.**

**Reference Diagram Q1A**

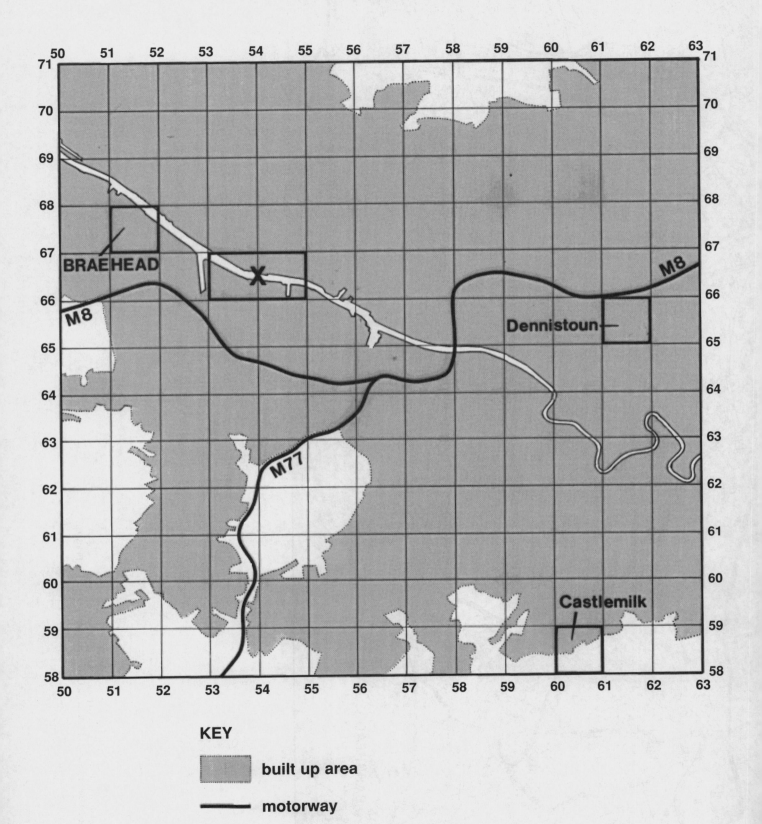

**KEY**

built up area

motorway

*Marks*

**1. (continued)**

Look at the Ordnance Survey Map Extract (No 1212/64) of the central Glasgow area and Reference Diagram Q1A on *Page two*.

(a)  Dennistoun (6165) and Castlemilk (6058) are both residential areas.

Using **map evidence**, describe the **differences** between these two areas.

_____

_____

_____

_____

_____

**4**

(b)  **Reference Diagram Q1B:  Braehead Shopping Centre**

Reference Diagram Q1B shows the recently built shopping centre at Braehead (5167).

Using **map evidence**, give reasons why it was built at this location.

_____

_____

_____

_____

**4**

**[Turn over**

DO NOT WRITE IN THIS MARGIN

KU | ES

*Marks*

**1. (continued)**

(c) Look at Reference Diagram Q1A and the map extract.

Give **map evidence** to show that area X (5366 and 5466), shown on Reference Diagram Q1A, is an industrial zone.

_____

_____

_____

_____

_____

4

(d) Reference Diagram Q1A shows the extension to the M77, opened in 1997.

Using **map evidence**, give the advantages **and** disadvantages of this new motorway.

Advantages _____

_____

_____

Disadvantages _____

_____

_____

4

*Marks*

**1. (continued)**

(*e*)

**Reference Text Q1C:
Selected Human Activities on River Clyde**

- Industry

- Communications

- Housing

- Recreation

Look at Reference Text Q1C and the map extract.

In what ways has the River Clyde both encouraged **and** restricted human activities in Glasgow?

_____

_____

_____

_____

_____

**4**

**[Turn over**

*Page five*

**[BLANK PAGE]**

*Marks*

2.    **Reference Diagram Q2:  Ox-Bow Lake**

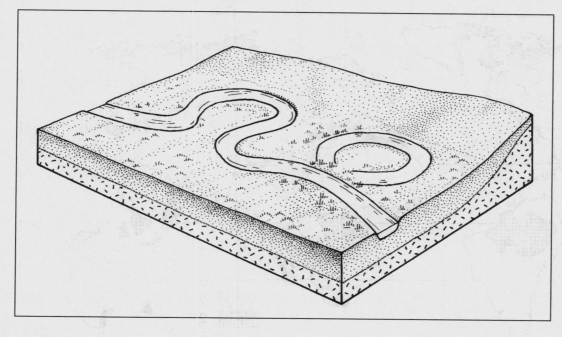

Explain how an ox-bow lake is formed.

You may use diagrams to illustrate your answer.

_____

_____

_____

_____

_____

_____

_____

_____

_____

**3**

**[Turn over**

**3.** **Reference Diagram Q3A: Selected Climate Regions**

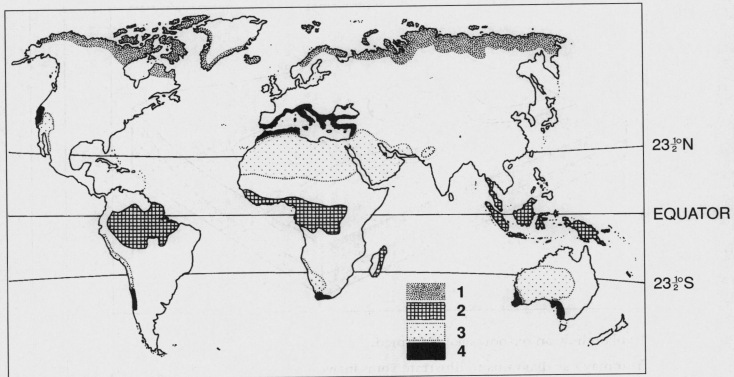

23½°N

EQUATOR

23½°S

1
2
3
4

KU | ES

*Marks*

(*a*)   Look at Reference Diagram Q3A.

Complete the table below by naming the climate regions **1** to **4** shown on the map.

Choose from:

Mediterranean, Tundra, Hot Desert, Equatorial Rain Forest.

| Number | Climate Region |
|--------|----------------|
| 1 | |
| 2 | |
| 3 | |
| 4 | |

3

*Marks*

## 3. (continued)

### Reference Diagram Q3B: Climate Graph

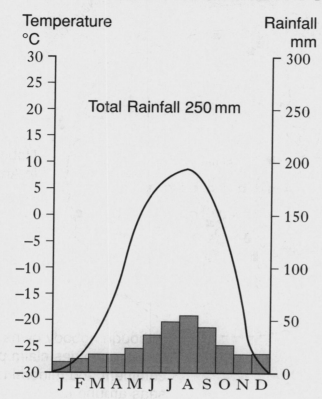

(b) Look at Reference Diagram Q3B.

The climate graph shows one of the four climates shown on Reference Diagram Q3A.

(i) Identify the climate shown by the graph.

Climate _____

**1**

(ii) Give reasons for your choice.

Reasons _____

_____

_____

_____

_____

**2**

[Turn over

4.

**Reference Diagram Q4A: Antarctica**

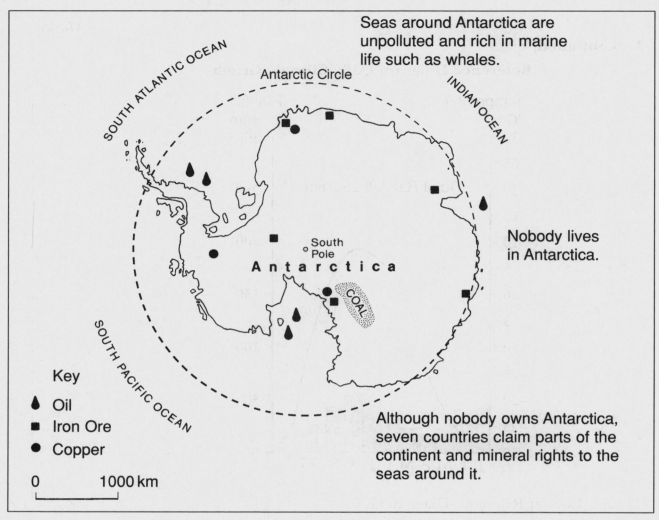

Seas around Antarctica are unpolluted and rich in marine life such as whales.

Nobody lives in Antarctica.

Although nobody owns Antarctica, seven countries claim parts of the continent and mineral rights to the seas around it.

Key
- Oil
- Iron Ore
- Copper

0          1000 km

**Reference Diagram Q4B: Different Views about the Antarctic Region**

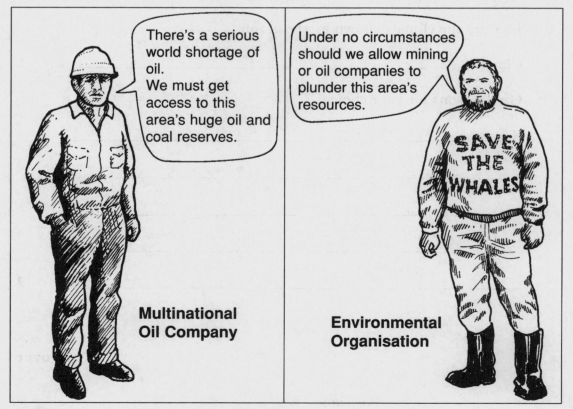

There's a serious world shortage of oil. We must get access to this area's huge oil and coal reserves.

**Multinational Oil Company**

Under no circumstances should we allow mining or oil companies to plunder this area's resources.

**Environmental Organisation**

DO NOT WRITE IN THIS MARGIN

| KU | ES |
|---|---|

*Marks*

**4. (continued)**

Look at Reference Diagrams Q4A and Q4B.

Do you think Antarctica's mineral resources should be developed?

Give reasons for your answer.

Tick (✓) your choice. YES ☐ NO ☐

Reasons ______________________________________________

______________________________________________

______________________________________________

______________________________________________

______________________________________________

______________________________________________

______________________________________________ 4

[Turn over

**5.**          **Reference Diagram Q5A:  Farming Landscape in 1950**

Small irregular fields

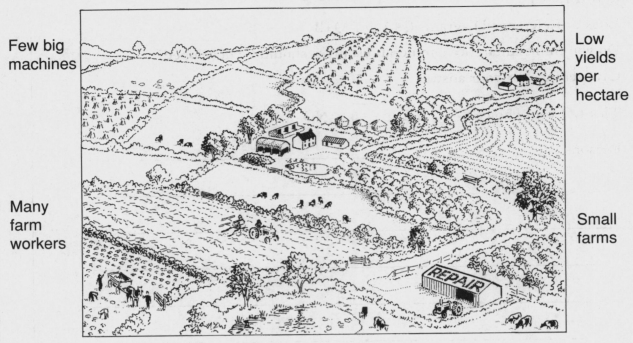

Few big
machines

Low
yields
per
hectare

Many
farm
workers

Small
farms

**Reference Diagram Q5B:  Farming Landscape in 2000**

Large regular fields

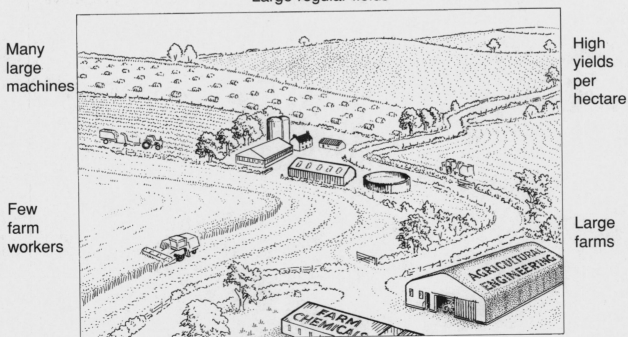

Many
large
machines

High
yields
per
hectare

Few
farm
workers

Large
farms

DO NOT WRITE IN THIS MARGIN

KU | ES

*Marks*

**5. (continued)**

(*a*) Look at Reference Diagrams Q5A and Q5B.

What are the advantages **and** disadvantages of the changes which have taken place in farming since 1950?

Advantages ______________________________

______________________________

______________________________

______________________________

Disadvantages ______________________________

______________________________

______________________________

______________________________ **4**

**[Turn over**

*Marks*

**5. (continued)**

**Reference Table Q5C: Farm Information collected by Student**

| Field Number | Field Size (hectares) | Slope Steepness (degrees) | Land Use |
|:---:|:---:|:---:|:---|
| 1 | 5 | 2 | barley |
| 2 | 7 | 12 | permanent grass |
| 3 | 8 | 4 | potatoes |
| 4 | 12 | 6 | barley |
| 5 | 13 | 20 | rough grazing |

**Reference Diagram Q5D: Map of Fields on Farm**

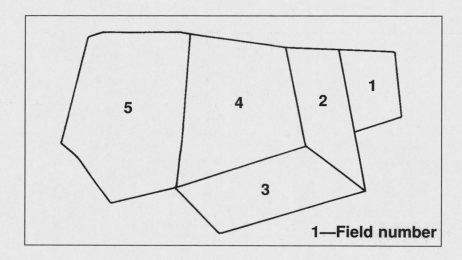

1—Field number

(b) Look at Reference Table Q5C and Reference Diagram Q5D.

Choose two **different** techniques to process the farm data that the student has collected.

Technique 1 _____

Technique 2 _____

Justify your choices. _____

_____

_____

_____

**4**

**6.**

### Reference Diagram Q6: Ben Lawers Area

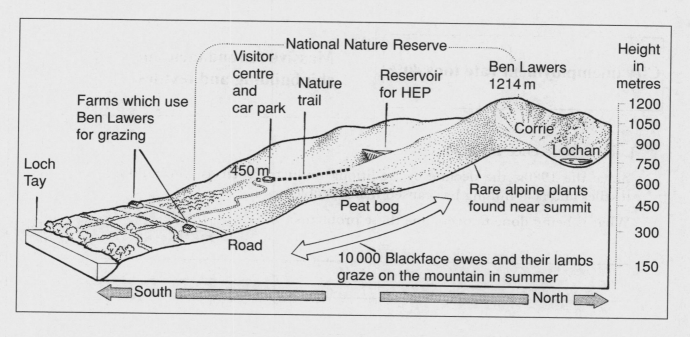

Look at Reference Diagram Q6.

(a) Many people visit Ben Lawers. What problems might this create for the area?

_____

_____

_____

_____

**4**

(b) A group of secondary pupils is to investigate the relationship between land use and height on Ben Lawers.

Describe **two** techniques which they could use to collect appropriate data.

Technique 1 _____

Technique 2 _____

Justify your choices. _____

_____

_____

_____

**4**

*Page fifteen*

**[Turn over**

*Marks*

DO NOT
WRITE IN
THIS
MARGIN

KU | ES

*Marks*

**7.** **Reference Diagram Q7: Newspaper Headlines of the 1980s**

| City unemployment rate tops 40% | **Massive redundancies in shipbuilding and textiles** |

Look at Reference Diagram Q7.

Since the 1980s, the decline of traditional industry such as shipbuilding, textiles and coal mining has caused many problems.

What is being done to overcome these problems?

_____

_____

_____

_____

3 _____

*Marks*

8. **Reference Diagram Q8:  Projected Changes in World Population**

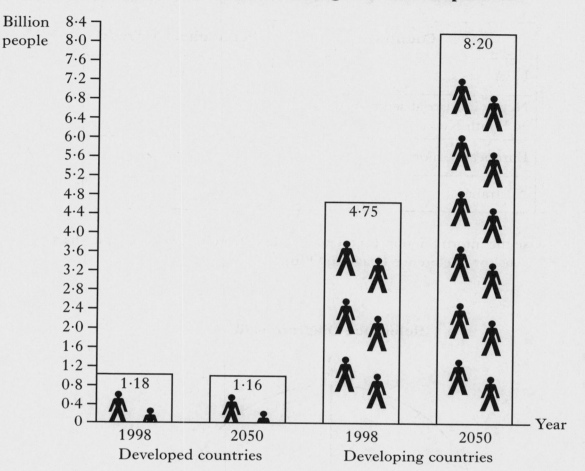

(a) Look at Reference Diagram Q8.

Describe in detail the changes in population predicted for the developed and developing countries.

_____

_____

_____

_____

**4**

(b) Describe the problems which **developing** countries are likely to have as a result of the changes in their population.

_____

_____

_____

_____

**4**

*Marks*

**9.** (*a*)       **Reference Table Q9A:  Japan—Main Export Partners**

| Country | Percentage of Trade |
|---|---|
| USA | 80 |
| Newly industrialised countries, eg South Korea | 10 |
| European Union | 5 |
| Australia | 5 |

Use the information in Reference Table Q9A to complete the pie chart below (Reference Diagram Q9B).

**3**

**Reference Diagram Q9B**

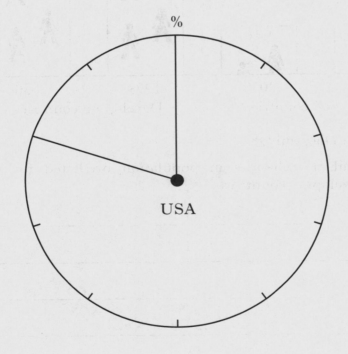

*Marks*

**9. (continued)**

(*b*)  **Reference Table Q9C:  Japan—Key Statistics**

| Selected Exports | World Rank | | |
|---|---|---|---|
| Car Manufacturing | 1 | Population (millions) 2000 | 130 |
| Computer Chips | 1 | Population (world rank) | 7 |
| Telecommunications | 1 | GNP (world rank) | 2 |
| Shipbuilding | 3 | | |
| Iron and Steel | 3 | | |

Look at the Reference Table Q9C.

Give reasons why Japan is one of the world's economic superpowers.

_____

_____

_____

_____

_____

4

**[Turn over for Question 10 on *Page twenty***

**10.** **Reference Text Q10A:  Problems of a Village in Mali, West Africa**

- very few children go to school
- mothers have to walk miles for water
- most people cannot read or write
- no rain, so the crops have died
- many babies ill or dying of hunger

**Reference Text Q10B:  Selected Types of Aid**

| Send emergency food and medicine | Set up a local school with trained teachers | Provide irrigation scheme |
|---|---|---|
| A | B | C |

Look at Reference Texts Q10A and Q10B above.

What type of aid do you think would be most suited to this village?

Tick (✓) your choice.

A ☐          B ☐          C ☐

Give reasons for your answer.

_____

_____

_____

_____

*Marks*

4

*[END OF QUESTION PAPER]*

**G**

FOR OFFICIAL USE

| | | | | | |
|---|---|---|---|---|---|

KU       ES

| | |
|---|---|

**Total Marks**

## 1260/403

NATIONAL
QUALIFICATIONS
2002

MONDAY, 13 MAY
10.25 AM–11.50 AM

## GEOGRAPHY
## STANDARD GRADE
General Level

---

**Fill in these boxes and read what is printed below.**

Full name of centre

Town

Forename(s)

Surname

Date of birth
Day   Month   Year       Scottish candidate number       Number of seat

1  Read the whole of each question carefully before you answer it.

2  Write in the spaces provided.

3  Where boxes like this ☐ are provided, put a tick ✓ in the box beside the answer you think
   is correct.

4  Try all the questions.

5  Do not give up the first time you get stuck:  you may be able to answer later questions.

6  Extra paper may be obtained from the invigilator, if required.

7  Before leaving the examination room you must give this book to the invigilator.  If you do
   not, you may lose all the marks for this paper.

SCOTTISH
QUALIFICATIONS
AUTHORITY

©

Extract No 1266/OLM14

1:25 000 Scale
Outdoor Leisure Series

Scale 1: 25 000

4 centimetres to 1 kilometre (one grid square)

Made and printed by Ordnance Survey 2001

© Crown copyright 1997

Ordnance Survey and the OS Symbol are registered trademarks and Outdoor Leisure is a trademark of Ordnance Survey, the national mapping agency of Great Britain. Reproduction in whole or in part by any means is prohibited without the prior written permission of Ordnance Survey. **For educational use only.**

1.

## Reference Diagram Q1A

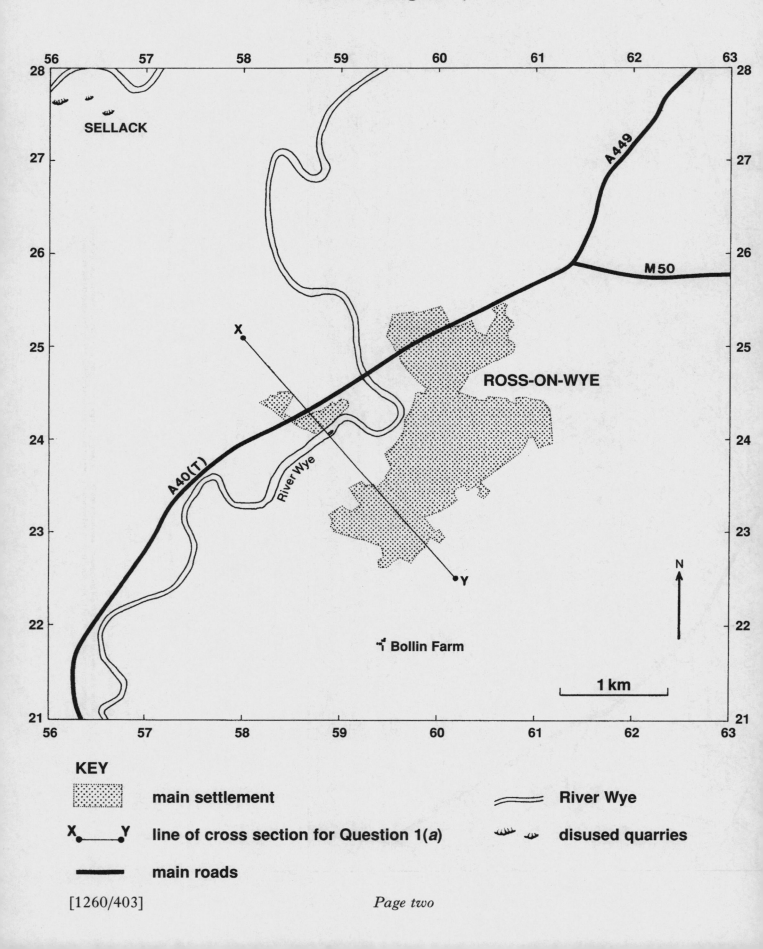

### KEY

| | | |
|---|---|---|
| main settlement | | River Wye |
| X———Y | line of cross section for Question 1(a) | disused quarries |
| | main roads | |

*Page two*

*Marks*

**1. (continued)**

Look at the Ordnance Survey Map Extract (No 1266/OLM14) of the Ross-on-Wye area and Reference Diagram Q1A on *Page two*.

**Reference Diagram Q1B: Cross-section from Claytons (580251) to the Fort (602225)**

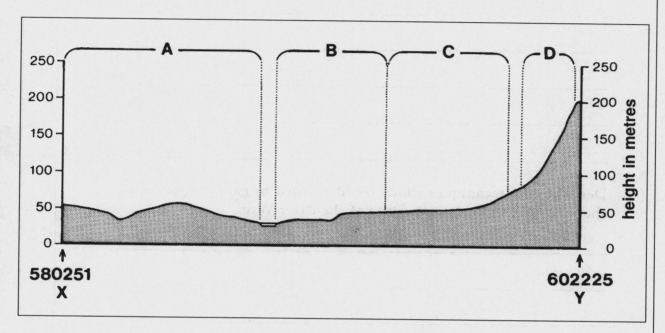

(a) Look at Reference Diagrams Q1A, Q1B and the OS Map.

Four areas of land use have been identified on the cross-section with letters A, B, C and D.

For each of the land uses listed below, write the correct letter from the cross-section in the space provided.

| Descriptions | Cross-section Letter |
|---|---|
| Outskirts of town | |
| Woodland | |
| Villages and farm land | |
| Pasture beside the river | |

3

[Turn over

Official SQA Past Papers: General Geography 2002

DO NOT
WRITE IN
THIS
MARGIN

KU | ES

*Marks*

**1. (continued)**

   (*b*)   Describe the **physical** features of the River Wye **and** its valley from where the river enters the map at 594280 to Wilton Bridge (590243).

        _____

        _____

        _____

        _____

        _____

        _____

**3**

   (*c*)   Describe **two** techniques which could be used to gather information about the **physical** characteristics of the River Wye.

        _____

        _____

        _____

        Why are these techniques suitable?

        _____

        _____

        _____

**4**

| KU | ES |
|----|----|

*Marks*

**1. (continued)**

(*d*)  Which type of farm is Bollin Farm 594218 likely to be?

Tick (✓) your choice.

Livestock ☐          Arable ☐          Mixed ☐

Give reasons to support your answer.

_____

_____

_____

_____

_____

_____

**3**

(*e*)  It is proposed to re-open and extend the quarries near Sellack in grid square 5627.

Do you agree or disagree with the proposal?

Give reasons for your answer.

_____

_____

_____

_____

_____

_____

**3**

**[Turn over**

DO NOT
WRITE IN
THIS
MARGIN

KU | ES

*Marks*

### 1. (continued)

(f) Using map evidence, describe the advantages **and** disadvantages of the site of the settlement of Ross-on-Wye.

Advantages _____

_____

_____

_____

Disadvantages _____

_____

_____

_____

**4**

(g) What is the **main** function of Ross-on-Wye?

Tick (✓) your choice.

Holiday resort ☐    Industrial town ☐    Market town ☐

Give map evidence to support your choice.

_____

_____

_____

_____

_____

_____

**4**

**[Turn over for Question 2 on *Page eight***

*Marks*

2.     **Reference Diagram Q2:  Area of Glacial Deposition**

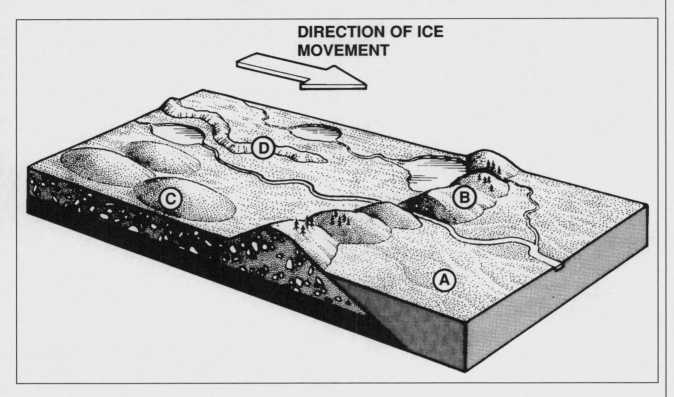

DIRECTION OF ICE
MOVEMENT

Look at Reference Diagram Q2.

(*a*)    Match each of the features of glacial deposition in the table to the
        correct letter (A, B, C, D) on the Reference Diagram.

| Feature | Letter |
|---|---|
| Drumlin | |
| Outwash Plain | |
| Esker | |
| Terminal Moraine | |

3

DO NOT WRITE IN THIS MARGIN

| KU | ES |
|---|---|

*Marks*

**2. (continued)**

(*b*) **Explain** how **one** of these features was formed. You may use a diagram to illustrate your answer.

Feature ______________________________

Explanation ____________________

____________________________________

____________________________________

____________________________________

____________________________________

____________________________________

____________________________________

____________________________________

____________________________________

____________________________________

____________________________________

**3**

**[Turn over**

**3.**

## Reference Diagram Q3A: Selected Climate Regions

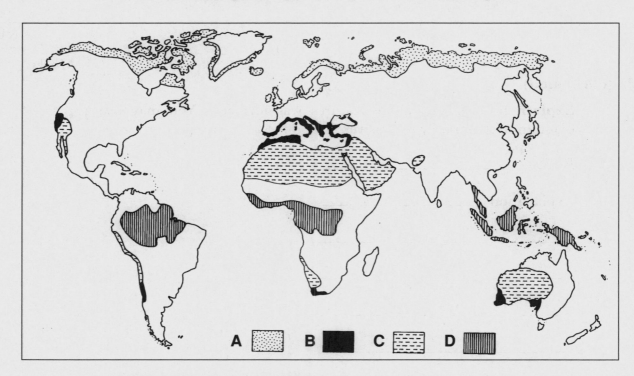

### Reference Diagram Q3B: Selected Climate Graphs

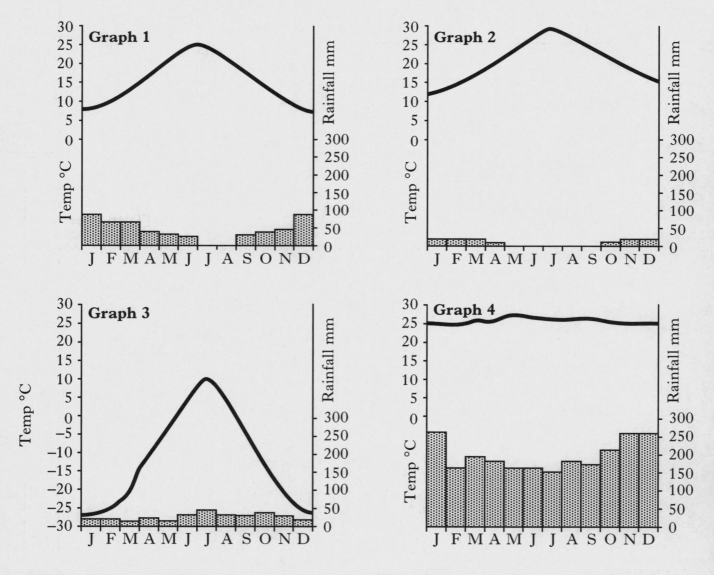

DO NOT WRITE IN THIS MARGIN

KU | ES

*Marks*

**3. (continued)**

Look at Reference Diagrams Q3A and Q3B.

(*a*) Complete the table below by adding the appropriate letter or number.

| Climate Type | Map Area | Graph |
|---|---|---|
| Hot Desert | C | |
| Equatorial Rainforest | | 4 |
| Mediterranean | B | |
| Tundra | | 3 |

3

(*b*) Describe **in detail** the main features of the climate shown in **Graph 3**.

3

**[Turn over**

*Marks*

4. **Reference Diagram Q4: Desertification**

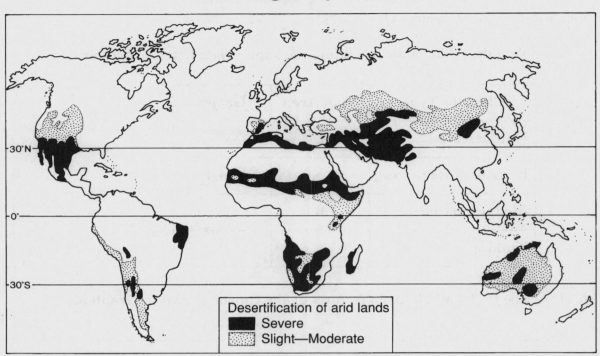

Desertification of arid lands
■ Severe
▒ Slight—Moderate

What are the main causes of desertification?

_____

_____

_____

_____

_____

_____

_____

3

**5.**

**Reference Diagram Q5A:**
**Relief in Scotland**

**Reference Diagram Q5B:  January**
**Temperatures in Scotland**

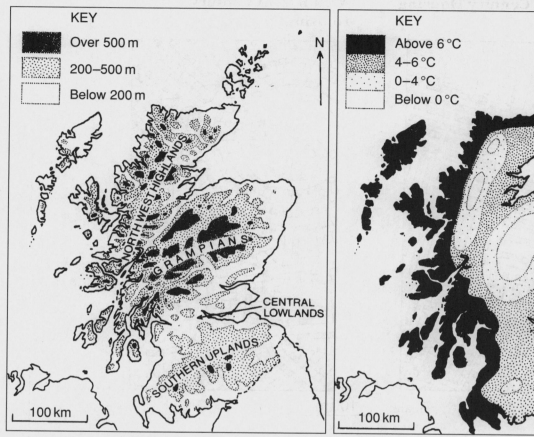

| KU | ES |
|----|----|

*Marks*

Look at Reference Diagrams Q5A and Q5B.

Describe in detail the relationship between relief and January temperatures
in Scotland.

_____

_____

_____

_____

_____

3

**[Turn over**

*Marks*

6.     **Reference Diagram Q6:  Two Housing Areas in Liverpool**

**Area A  19th Century Housing**          **Area B  20th Century Housing**

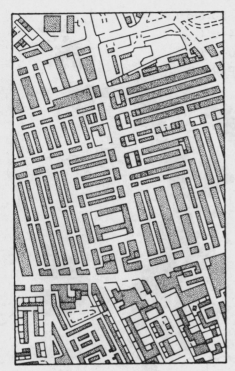
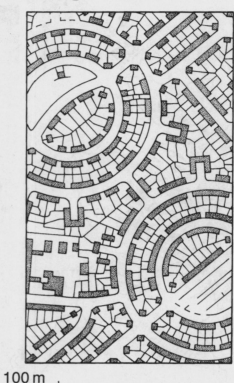

Scale: |⎯ **100 m** ⎯|

Look at the areas A and B above.

(*a*)  Describe the differences in housing density and street patterns between the two areas.

_____

_____

_____

_____

_____

**3**

DO NOT WRITE IN THIS MARGIN

| | KU | ES |
|---|---|---|

*Marks*

**6. (continued)**

(*b*) Describe **two** techniques you could use to gather information in areas A and B to show differences in quality of environment.

Give reasons for your choice.

4

**[Turn over**

**7.** **Reference Diagram Q7: Doxford International Business and Technology Park**

SUNDERLAND HEALTH AND RACQUET CLUB    HOUSING ESTATES    FINISHED PREMISES AVAILABLE    LAND FOR DEVELOPMENT    A19 DUAL CARRIAGEWAY

A690 DUAL CARRIAGEWAY LINK TO A1(M) MOTORWAY    ENTERPRISE ZONE    EARTH SATELLITE STATION

Marks

**7. (continued)**

(a) A business and technology park is a planned industrial area for offices and hi-tech industries.

Study Reference Diagram Q7.

Describe the advantages of the Doxford International Business and Technology Park **for the companies** located there.

_____

_____

_____

_____

_____

_____

**4**

(b) Describe the advantages **for older industrial areas** such as Sunderland of having many modern companies located nearby.

_____

_____

_____

_____

_____

_____

**4**

**[Turn over**

**8.**   **Reference Table Q8:  Urban Population as a percentage of
Total Population**

|  | **1950** | **1970** | **1990** | **2000** |
|---|---|---|---|---|
| **India** | 17 | 20 | 28 | 34 |

Look at Reference Table Q8.

(a)   Give reasons for the changes in the percentage of urban population of Developing countries such as India.

_____

_____

_____

_____

_____

**4**

(b)   Give **one** processing technique which could be used to show the information in Reference Table Q8.  Give reasons for your choice.

_____

_____

_____

_____

_____

_____

_____

**3**

*Marks*

9. **Reference Diagram Q9: Government considering entry to a Trade Alliance**

Look at Reference Diagram Q9.

What are the advantages **and** disadvantages for countries which are members of a Trading Alliance?

_____

_____

_____

_____

_____

_____

4

**[Turn over for Question 10 on *Page twenty***

*Marks*

**10.** **Reference Diagram Q10: Examples of Intermediate Technology**

**Village biogas plant** takes all waste and provides gas for fuel and fertiliser for crops.

Waste

INLET

OUTLET Gas

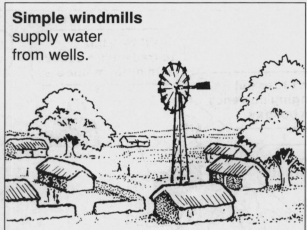

**Simple windmills** supply water from wells.

Look at Reference Diagram Q10.

Explain why intermediate technology, such as that shown in Reference Diagram Q10, is suitable for many rural communities in Developing countries.

_____

_____

_____

_____

_____

_____

_____

4

*[END OF QUESTION PAPER]*

**G**

FOR OFFICIAL USE

| | | | | | |
|---|---|---|---|---|---|

| KU | ES |
|---|---|
| | |

Total Marks

# 1260/403

NATIONAL
QUALIFICATIONS
2003

THURSDAY, 15 MAY
10.25 AM–11.50 AM

# GEOGRAPHY
## STANDARD GRADE
General Level

**Fill in these boxes and read what is printed below.**

Full name of centre

Town

Forename(s)

Surname

Date of birth
Day Month Year     Scottish candidate number     Number of seat

1 Read the whole of each question carefully before you answer it.

2 Write in the spaces provided.

3 Where boxes like this ☐ are provided, put a tick ✓ in the box beside the answer you think is correct.

4 Try all the questions.

5 Do not give up the first time you get stuck: you may be able to answer later questions.

6 Extra paper may be obtained from the invigilator, if required.

7 Before leaving the examination room you must give this book to the invigilator. If you do not, you may lose all the marks for this paper.

SCOTTISH
QUALIFICATIONS
AUTHORITY

©

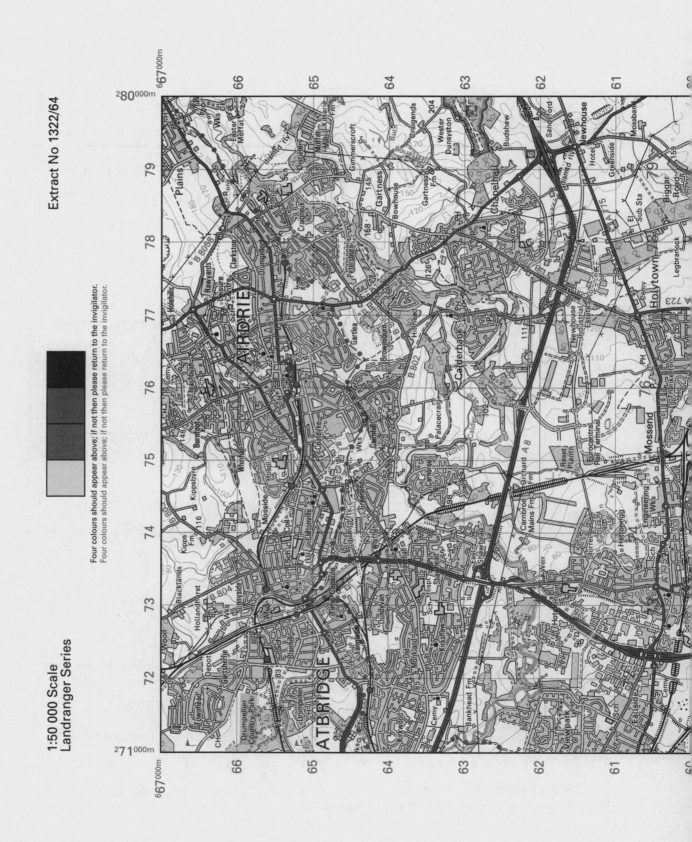

1:50 000 Scale
Landranger Series

Extract No 1322/64

Four colours should appear above; if not then please return to the invigilator.
Four colours should appear above; if not then please return to the invigilator.

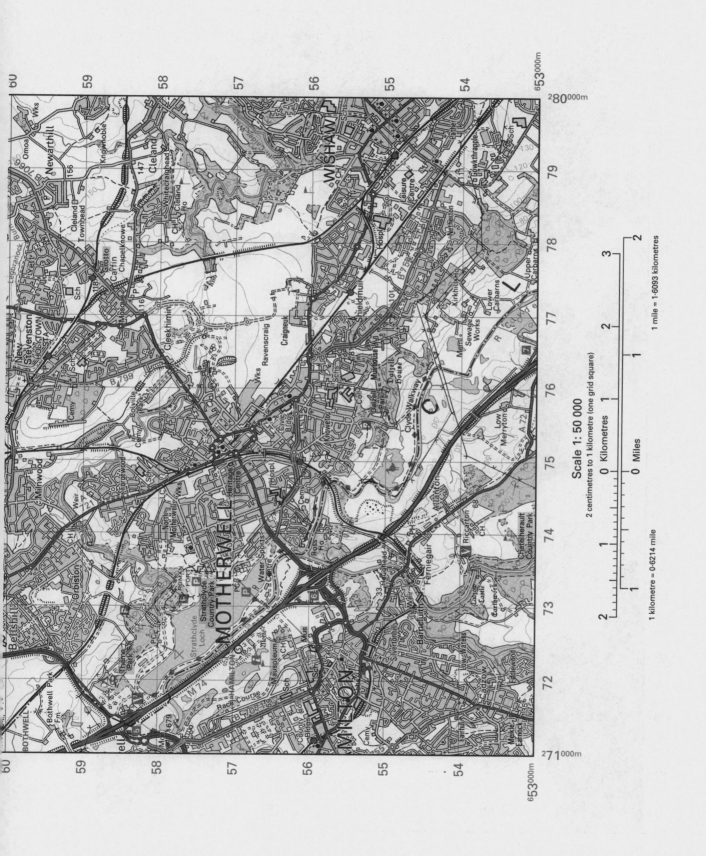

Scale 1: 50 000

2 centimetres to 1 kilometre (one grid square)

**1.**

## Reference Diagram Q1A

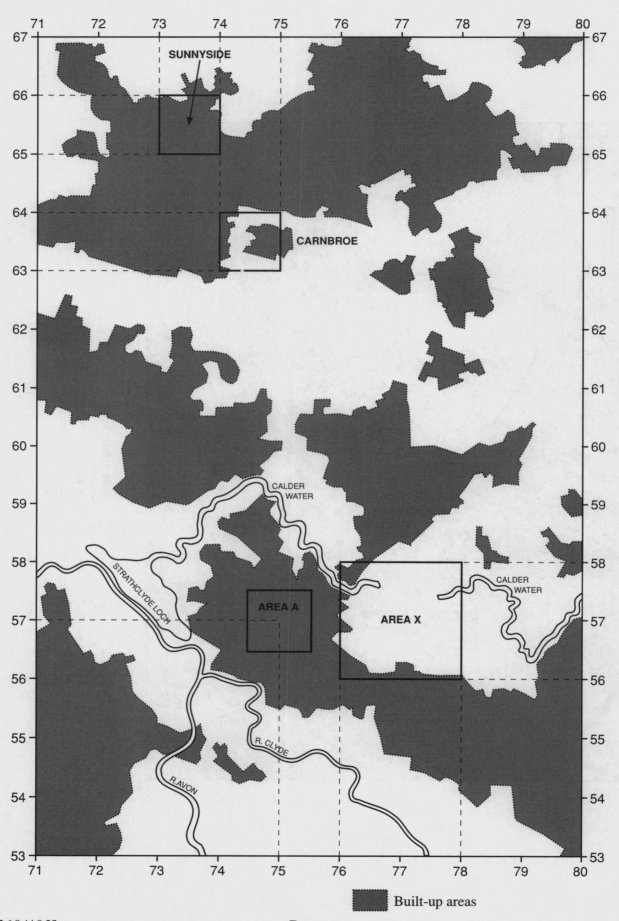

■ Built-up areas

**1. (continued)**

Look at the Ordnance Survey Map Extract (No 1322/64) and at Reference Diagram Q1A on *Page two*.

(*a*) Give map evidence to show that the CBD of Motherwell is in Area A.

_____

_____

_____

**3**

(*b*) Two residential areas of Coatbridge are found in squares 7365 (Sunnyside) and 7463 (Carnbroe).

**Describe** the differences between these areas, referring to map evidence.

_____

_____

_____

_____

_____

**4**

(*c*) Find Bankhead Farm at 713630.

Using map evidence, describe the advantages **and** disadvantages of its location.

_____

_____

_____

_____

_____

**4**

**[Turn over**

*Marks*

**1. (continued)**

**Reference Diagram Q1B: An old Ordnance Survey Map of part of Motherwell (1950 edition)**

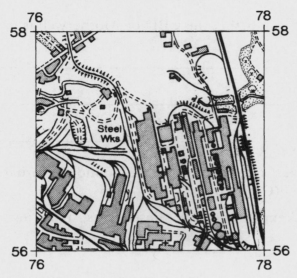

(*d*)  (i)  The area shown on the diagram above is identified as Area X on Reference Diagram Q1A.

Look at the Ordnance Survey Extract **and** the old Ordnance Survey Map above.

Describe the changes which have taken place between 1950 and the present day.

_____

_____

_____

_____

**3**

(ii)  Comparing old and new maps is one technique for gathering data on land use.

State **two other** techniques that local pupils could use to gather information about land use change in this industrial area.

Give reasons for your choice.

Technique one  _____

Technique two  _____

Reasons  _____

_____

_____

_____

**4**

*Marks*

## 1. (continued)

(e) Strathclyde Country Park is centred on Strathclyde Loch.

Using map evidence, describe the attractions which this park has for visitors.

_____

_____

_____

_____

_____

**3**

(f) Describe the **physical** features of the River Clyde **and** its valley between 774530 and 737560.

_____

_____

_____

_____

_____

**4**

**[Turn over**

**2.** **Reference Diagram Q2: Landscapes of the Tay Valley**

**Q2A: Upper Course of the River Tay**

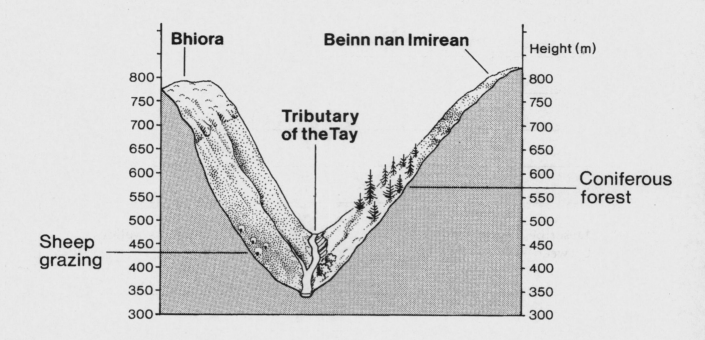

**Q2B: Lower Course of the River Tay**

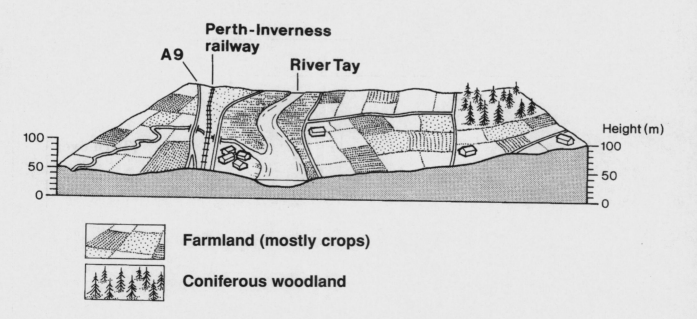

DO NOT WRITE IN THIS MARGIN

| KU | ES |
|---|---|

*Marks*

**2. (continued)**

(*a*) Look at the landscapes shown in the Reference Diagram opposite.

Compare the **physical** features of the River Tay and its valley in the two diagrams.

4

(*b*) **Explain** why land use along the River Tay is different in the two diagrams.

4

[Turn over

*Marks*

3.    **Reference Diagram Q3A:  Features of a Stevenson Screen**

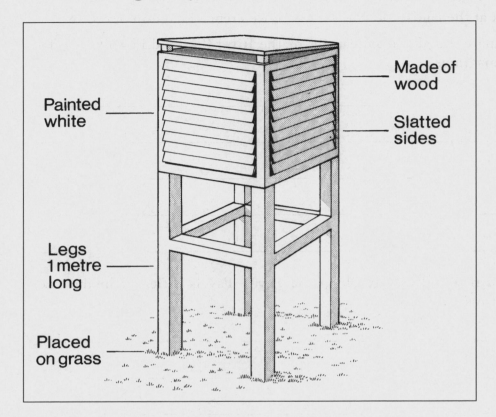

Painted white

Made of wood

Slatted sides

Legs 1 metre long

Placed on grass

(a)    Look at Reference Diagram Q3A which shows some design features of a Stevenson Screen which is used to house thermometers.

Choose **three** of these features and for each **explain** why it is necessary.

First Feature Chosen _____

Explanation _____

_____

Second Feature Chosen _____

Explanation _____

_____

Third Feature Chosen _____

Explanation _____

_____

3

*Marks*

**3. (continued)**

**Reference Diagram Q3B: Weather Map of Mainland Scotland on
25 November 2001**

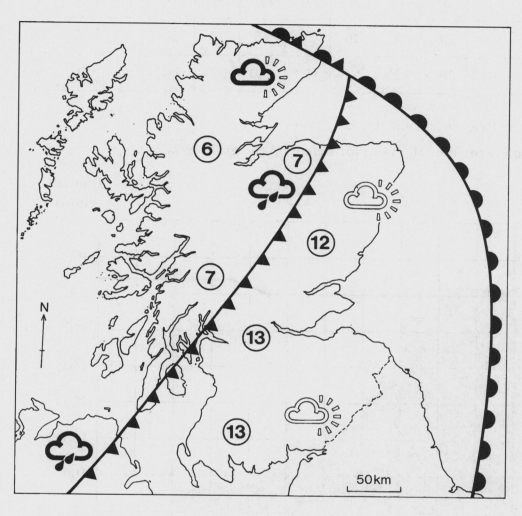

(b)  Look at Reference Diagram Q3B.

Give reasons for the variations in temperatures throughout Scotland
on 25 November.

_____

_____

_____

_____

_____

_____

_____

**3**

*Marks*

**4.**           **Reference Table Q4A:  Climate Statistics for Belem, Brazil**

| | J | F | M | A | M | J | J | A | S | O | N | D |
|---|---|---|---|---|---|---|---|---|---|---|---|---|
| Temperature (°C) | 27 | 26 | 26 | 26 | 26 | 26 | 26 | 26 | 27 | 27 | 27 | 27 |
| Rainfall (mm) | 320 | 360 | 360 | 320 | 260 | 170 | 150 | 110 | 90 | 80 | 70 | 160 |

(*a*)    Look at Reference Table Q4A.

Complete the rainfall graph for Belem on the grid below.

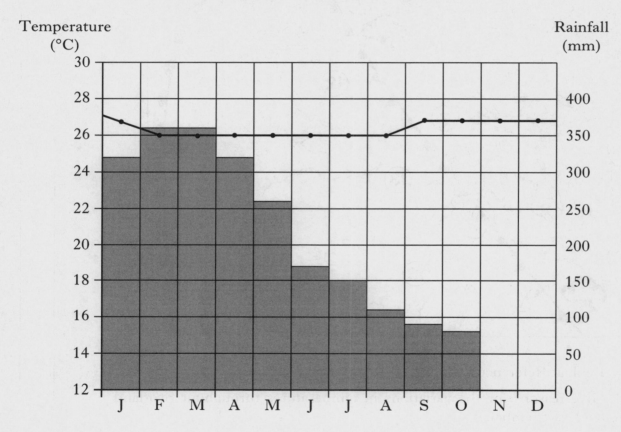

2

(*b*)    Describe in detail the climate of Belem.

_____

_____

_____

_____

_____

4

**4. (continued)**

**Reference Diagram Q4B: Causes of Deforestation in Brazil**

Trans Amazon Highway

Cattle Ranching

Open-Cast Iron Ore Mine

*Marks*

(c)   Look at Reference Diagram Q4B above.

Describe the effects of the activities shown in the diagram on the environment **and** people of Brazil's rainforest.

_____

_____

_____

_____

_____

_____

**4**

**[Turn over**

5. **Reference Diagram Q5A:
Needs for a Modern Port**

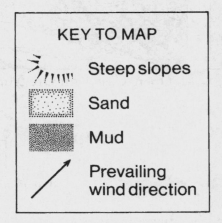

- **Flat land**
- **Deep water**
- **Shelter**
- **Close to city**

KEY TO MAP

- Steep slopes
- Sand
- Mud
- Prevailing wind direction

**Reference Diagram Q5B:
Potential Sites for a Modern Port**

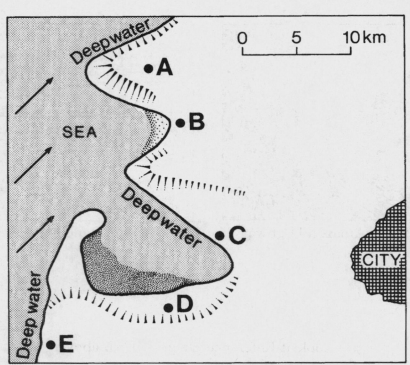

KU | ES

*Marks*

Look at Reference Diagrams Q5A and Q5B.

Which site—**A**, **B**, **C**, **D** or **E**—is the best for a modern port?

Choice _____

Give reasons for your answer.

_____

_____

_____

_____

_____

4

DO NOT
WRITE IN
THIS
MARGIN

KU | ES

*Marks*

**6.** **Reference Diagram Q6A: Migration from Rural Areas in Developing Countries**

(a) Look at Reference Diagram Q6A.

People living in rural areas in developing countries can face many problems which may encourage them to migrate to cities.

Describe the type of problems found in such rural areas.

_____

_____

_____

_____

_____

_____

**4**

**[Turn over**

**6. (continued)**

**Reference Diagram Q6B: Migrants' View of Life in a Developing City**

*(b)* Look at Reference Diagram Q6B.

Do you think people benefit by moving from the countryside to the city?

Explain your answer.

*Marks*

7. **Reference Diagram Q7:** **Headquarters of the World's 100 Largest Companies**

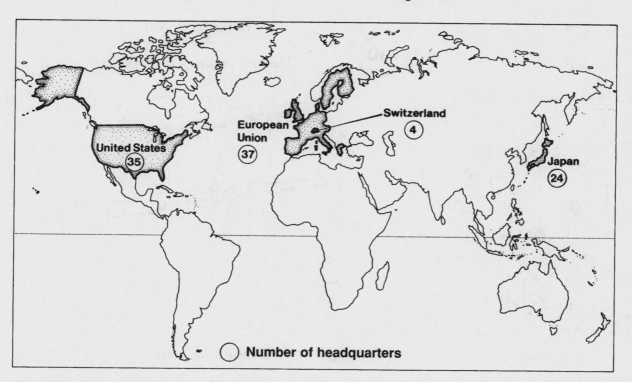

Number of headquarters

Look at Reference Diagram Q7 above.

(*a*) Give reasons for the location of the world's 100 largest companies.

_____

_____

_____

_____

_____

3

(*b*) Give **one other** technique that could be used to process the information shown on the map.

Give reasons for your choice.

_____

_____

_____

_____

_____

3

*Page fifteen* **[Turn over for Question 8 on *Page sixteen***

*Marks*

**8.** **Reference Diagram Q8: Aid to Developing Countries**

| Short-term Aid | | Long-term Aid |
|---|---|---|
| Immediate help | **AID** | Helps a country to develop |

- Clean water
- Food
- Emergency shelter
- Medicines

- Rebuilding homes
- Road building
- Electricity network
- Building hospitals

Look at Reference Diagram Q8.

Which type of aid, short-term or long-term, would be most useful to a **developing** country after an earthquake?

Give reasons for your answer.

_____

_____

_____

_____

_____

4

[*END OF QUESTION PAPER*]

**C**

## 1260/105

SCOTTISH
CERTIFICATE OF
EDUCATION
1999

TUESDAY, 11 MAY
10.45 AM – 12.45 PM

GEOGRAPHY
STANDARD GRADE
Credit Level

All questions should be attempted.

Candidates should read the questions carefully. Answers should be clearly expressed and relevant.

Credit will always be given for appropriate sketch-maps and diagrams.

Write legibly and neatly, and leave a space of about one cm between the lines.

Marks may be deducted for bad spelling and bad punctuation, and for writing that is difficult to read.

All maps and diagrams in this paper have been printed in black only: no other colours have been used.

SCOTTISH
QUALIFICATIONS
AUTHORITY

1:50 000 Scale
Landranger Series

Four colours should appear above; if not then please return to the invigilator.
Four colours should appear above; if not then please return to the invigilator.

Extract No 1138/90

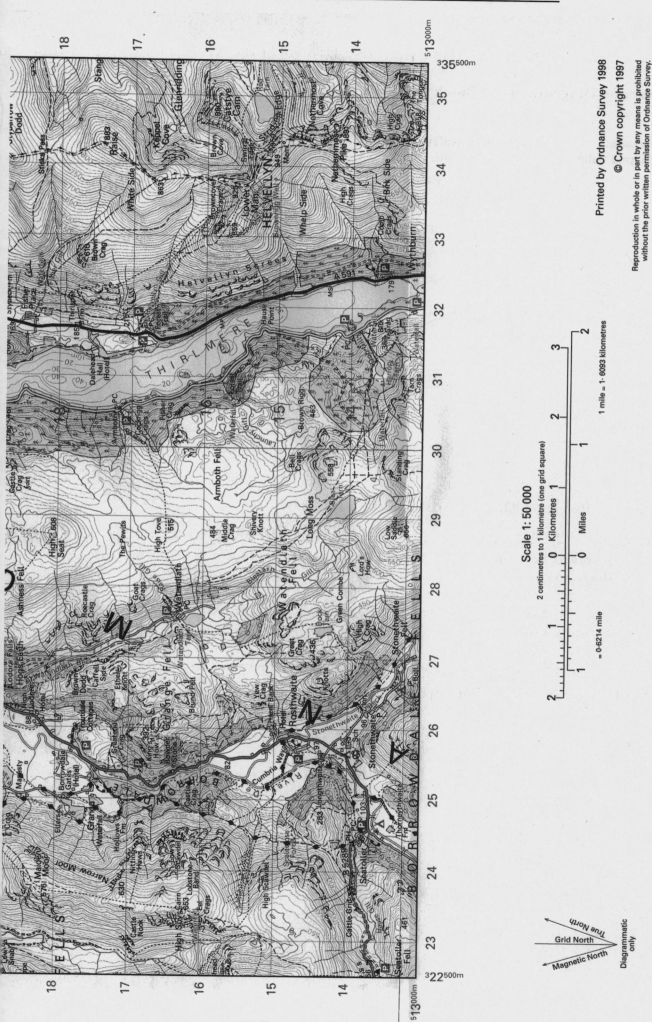

Scale 1:50 000

2 centimetres to 1 kilometre (one grid square)

1 mile = 1·6093 kilometres

= 0·6214 mile

Printed by Ordnance Survey 1998

© Crown copyright 1997

Reproduction in whole or in part by any means is prohibited
without the prior written permission of Ordnance Survey.

Map reproduced from Ordnance Survey mapping with the permission of the
Controller of Her Majesty's Stationery Office, © Crown copyright, Licence No. 100036009.

Diagrammatic
only

True North

Grid North

Magnetic North

**1.** This question refers to the OS Map Extract (No 1138/90) of the Keswick area.

**Reference Diagram Q1A: Block Diagram of Map Extract South of Northing 17**

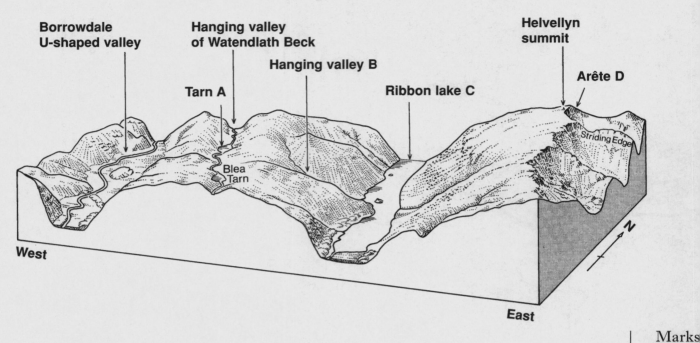

| | Marks |
|---|---|
| | KU | |

(*a*) Look at Reference Diagram Q1A and the map extract.

   (i)   Give the names of Tarn A, Hanging Valley B, Ribbon Lake C and Arête D.   **3**

   (ii)   **Explain** how **one** of the features listed below was formed. You may use diagrams to illustrate your answer.

       Borrowdale U-shaped valley, Hanging Valley of Watendlath Beck, Striding Edge Arête.   **4**

(*b*) Find the area shown by Reference Diagram Q1B on the map extract.

   **Explain** the distribution of population as indicated by the settlement map.

**1. (continued)**

### Reference Diagram Q1B: Distribution of Settlement

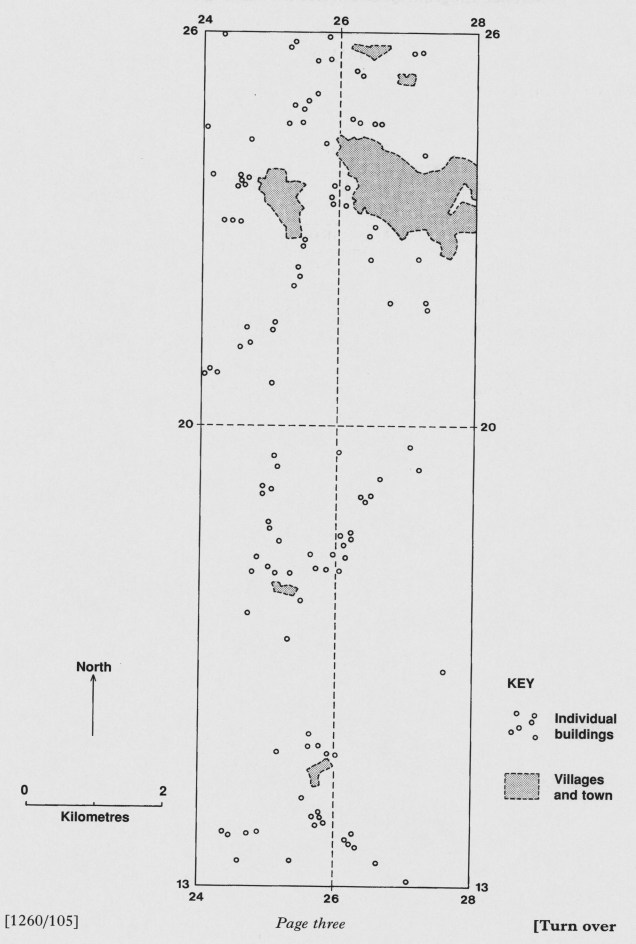

North

KEY

○ ○
○ ○  Individual
○ ○   buildings

▒ Villages
and town

0 ———————— 2
Kilometres

Marks
KU  F

**1. (continued)**

**Reference Diagram Q1C:  Factors influencing Tourism**

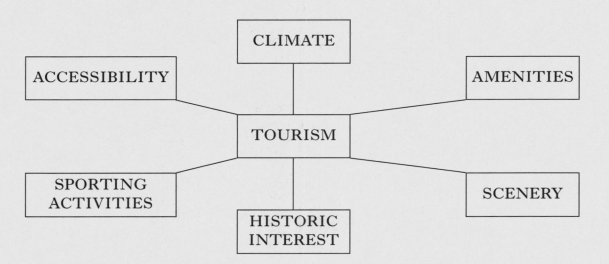

(c)   (i)   Look at Reference Diagram Q1C and the map extract.

Using map evidence, describe the advantages **and** disadvantages of Keswick as a holiday resort.

(ii)   Describe in detail two gathering techniques you would use to assess the economic **and** environmental impact of tourism in and around Keswick.

Justify your choice of techniques.

2. **Reference Diagram Q2: Field Sketch of the Upper Course of a Valley**

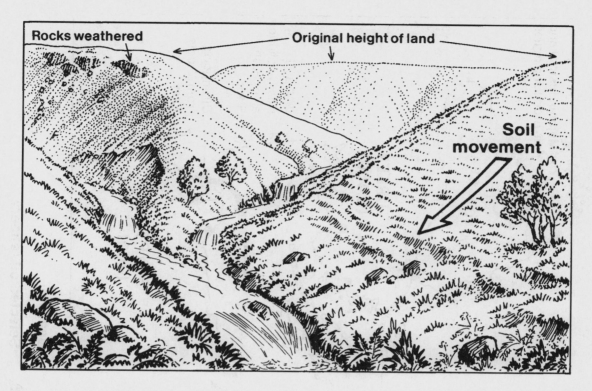

Look at the Reference Diagram Q2 above.

**Explain** how the V-shaped valley was formed.

4

**[Turn over**

3.

Reference Diagram Q3A: Pollution in the Mediterranean

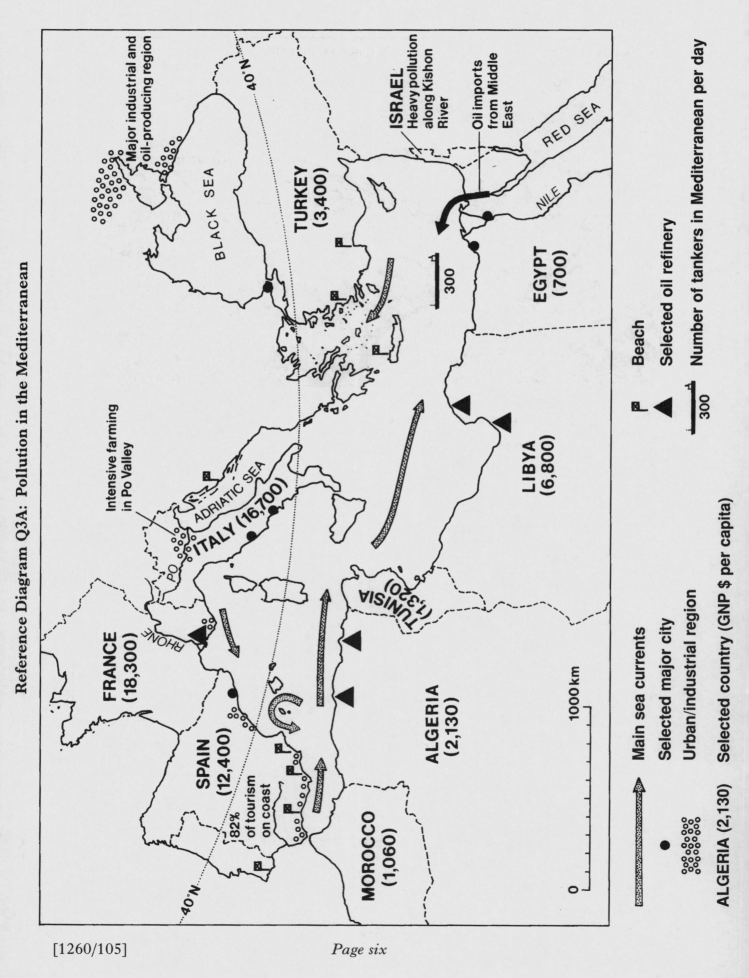

Marks
KU | E

## 3. (continued)

### Reference Diagram Q3B: Expected Population Growth of the Mediterranean Coastal Regions

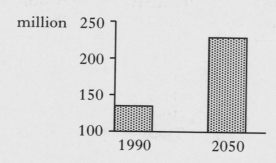

### Reference Diagram Q3C: Sources of Pollution in the Mediterranean

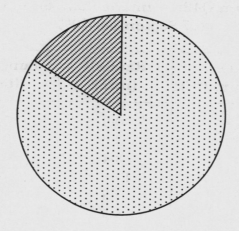

 pollution originating from activities on land

pollution originating from activities at sea

Look at Reference Diagrams Q3A, Q3B and Q3C.

(a) **Explain** why the Mediterranean Sea suffers from severe pollution.

6

(b) "Solving the Mediterranean's pollution problem requires international cooperation. We have a common interest. All Mediterranean countries, rich and poor, will have to make sacrifices to clean up and protect the Mediterranean. Penalties for chemical pollution must be tough!"

(Spokesperson for Environmental Organisation)

What are the arguments for **and** against accepting the proposals to solve the Mediterranean's pollution problem?

4

**[Turn over**

Marks

KU | E

**4.** **Reference Diagram Q4A: Climatic Data for Glasgow Airport**
**1–7 September 1997**

| Date | Average Temperature (°C) | Rainfall (mm) | Sunshine (hrs) | Wind Direction |
|------|--------------------------|---------------|----------------|----------------|
| 1 | 14·4 | 0·9 | 3·7 | W |
| 2 | 12·1 | 12·6 | 1·0 | S |
| 3 | 16·8 | 11·3 | 1·7 | S |
| 4 | 14·5 | 10·4 | 8·3 | SW |
| 5 | 14·7 | Trace | 4·1 | SW |
| 6 | 13·5 | 1·6 | 4·0 | SW |
| 7 | 15·1 | 0·4 | 0·0 | W |

**Reference Diagram Q4B: Climatic data for Stornoway Airport**
**1–7 September 1997**

| Date | Average Temperature (°C) | Rainfall (mm) | Sunshine (hrs) | Wind Direction |
|------|--------------------------|---------------|----------------|----------------|
| 1 | 15·2 | 0·9 | 5·0 | NW |
| 2 | 13·2 | 3·9 | 0·8 | S |
| 3 | 13·6 | 8·4 | 1·1 | S |
| 4 | 12·4 | 19·1 | 2·6 | S |
| 5 | 12·0 | 7·8 | 0·1 | W |
| 6 | 12·4 | 5·5 | 0·4 | W |
| 7 | 13·3 | 3·8 | 0·0 | SW |

Look at Reference Diagrams Q4A and Q4B.

Which processing techniques would you use to **compare** the statistics for the two airports?

Justify your choice of techniques.

Marks
KU | E

**3. (continued)**

### Reference Diagram Q3B: Expected Population Growth of the Mediterranean Coastal Regions

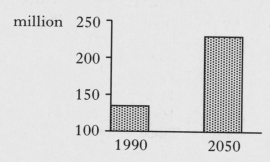

### Reference Diagram Q3C: Sources of Pollution in the Mediterranean

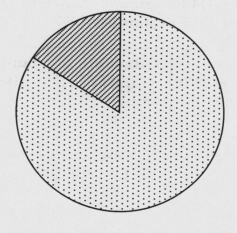

 pollution originating from activities on land

pollution originating from activities at sea

Look at Reference Diagrams Q3A, Q3B and Q3C.

(a) **Explain** why the Mediterranean Sea suffers from severe pollution.

6

(b) "Solving the Mediterranean's pollution problem requires international cooperation. We have a common interest. All Mediterranean countries, rich and poor, will have to make sacrifices to clean up and protect the Mediterranean. Penalties for chemical pollution must be tough!"

(Spokesperson for Environmental Organisation)

What are the arguments for **and** against accepting the proposals to solve the Mediterranean's pollution problem?

4

**[Turn over**

Marks

| | KU | E |

**4.**  **Reference Diagram Q4A:  Climatic Data for Glasgow Airport**
**1–7 September 1997**

| Date | Average Temperature (°C) | Rainfall (mm) | Sunshine (hrs) | Wind Direction |
|------|--------------------------|---------------|----------------|----------------|
| 1 | 14·4 | 0·9 | 3·7 | W |
| 2 | 12·1 | 12·6 | 1·0 | S |
| 3 | 16·8 | 11·3 | 1·7 | S |
| 4 | 14·5 | 10·4 | 8·3 | SW |
| 5 | 14·7 | Trace | 4·1 | SW |
| 6 | 13·5 | 1·6 | 4·0 | SW |
| 7 | 15·1 | 0·4 | 0·0 | W |

**Reference Diagram Q4B:  Climatic data for Stornoway Airport**
**1–7 September 1997**

| Date | Average Temperature (°C) | Rainfall (mm) | Sunshine (hrs) | Wind Direction |
|------|--------------------------|---------------|----------------|----------------|
| 1 | 15·2 | 0·9 | 5·0 | NW |
| 2 | 13·2 | 3·9 | 0·8 | S |
| 3 | 13·6 | 8·4 | 1·1 | S |
| 4 | 12·4 | 19·1 | 2·6 | S |
| 5 | 12·0 | 7·8 | 0·1 | W |
| 6 | 12·4 | 5·5 | 0·4 | W |
| 7 | 13·3 | 3·8 | 0·0 | SW |

Look at Reference Diagrams Q4A and Q4B.

Which processing techniques would you use to **compare** the statistics for the two airports?

Justify your choice of techniques.

5.     Reference Diagram Q5:  Oykell Farm in the Northwest Highlands

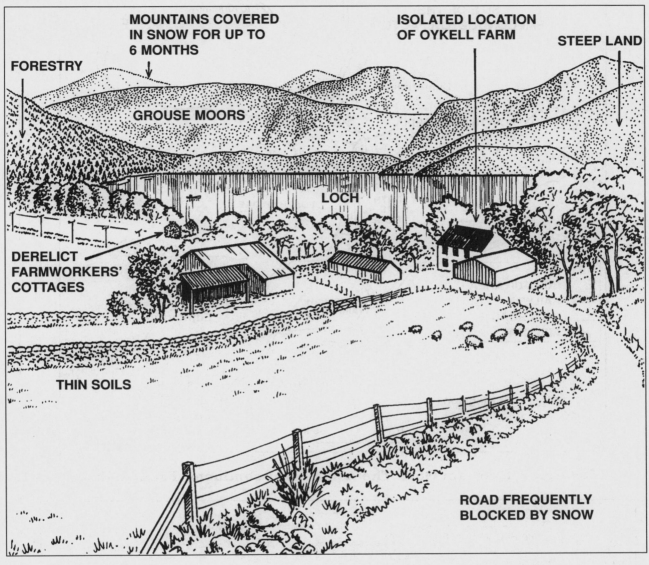

| | | Marks | |
| --- | --- | --- | --- |
| | | KU | ES |

Look at Reference Diagram Q5.

Oykell Farm experiences a number of difficulties due to the climate, the type of land and its location in the Northwest Highlands.

**Explain** the decisions which the farmer could take to overcome these difficulties and to ensure a reasonable income from the farm.

You must refer to both farming **and** non-farming activities.

6

**6.**

### Reference Diagram Q6A: Location of an Asian Electronics Semi-conductor Factory

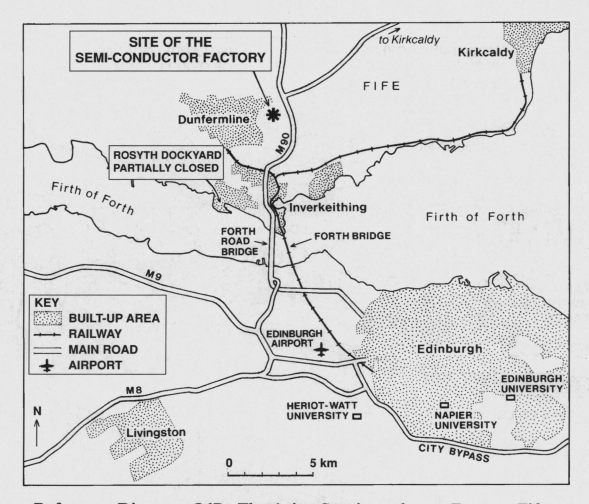

### Reference Diagram Q6B: The Asian Semi-conductor Factory, Fife

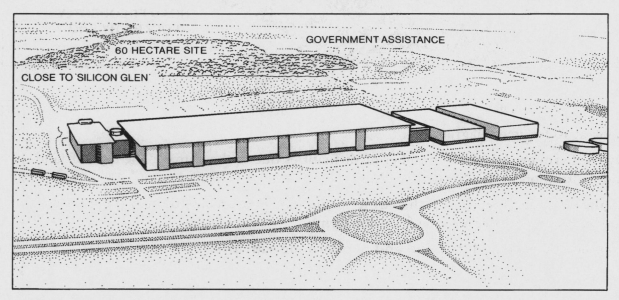

Study Reference Diagrams Q6A and Q6B.

In 1997, an Asian electronics company built a new factory near Dunfermline to produce computer chips (semi-conductors).

**Explain** the advantages of this site and its location in Fife **for** the company.

6

7. **Reference Diagram Q7A: Percentage Growth of World Trade Share for Selected Countries 1980–1992**

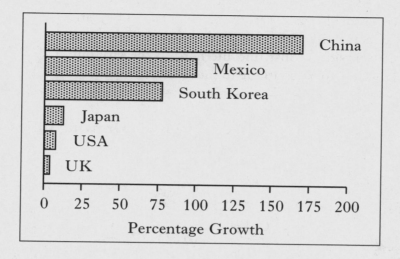

**Reference Table Q7B: Selected Statistics for China, Japan and USA 1992**

| | China | Japan | USA |
|---|---|---|---|
| Land area (sq km) | 9 596 960 | 377 800 | 9 809 431 |
| Population (million) | 1185 | 125 | 264 |
| World trade figures (million US dollars) | 165 000 | 572 000 | 1 000 000 |
| Literacy (percentage) | 70 | 99 | 99 |
| Labour Costs (US dollars per hour) | 1 | 16·5 | 16 |

Look at Reference Diagram Q7A and Reference Table Q7B.

"Japan and USA are currently dominant in international relations and trade. However, by the year 2020, China will have overtaken both Japan and USA."

Do you agree with this statement? Give reasons for your answer.

5

**[Turn over**

Marks

KU | E

**8.**

### Reference Text Q8A

> "In Developing countries people leave the countryside for a variety of reasons. They are attracted by the city and pushed from the countryside. Most find life hard in the city but large numbers continue to move there."

### Reference Diagram Q8B: The Ten Fastest Growing Cities

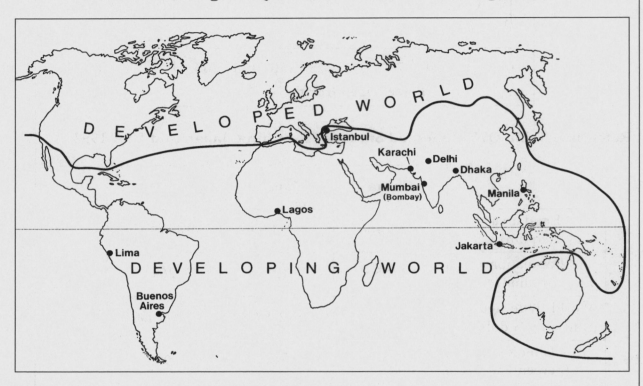

### Reference Text Q8C: Problems of Fast Growing Cities in the Developing Countries

> Higher living costs
>
> Not enough formal jobs
>
> Shortage of good housing
>
> Pollution and overcrowding

Marks

| KU | E |
|---|---|

**8. (continued)**

Study Reference Texts Q8A and Q8C and Reference Diagram Q8B.

(a) Despite the problems outlined in Reference Text Q8C, large numbers of people in **Developing** Countries are still moving from the countryside to the cities. **Explain** why this is happening.

6

(b) In **Developed** countries the population in many large cities such as Chicago and London is static or falling.

Give reasons for this.

4

**[Turn over**

Marks
KU    E

**9.    Reference Diagram Q9:  Two Approaches to Development in India**

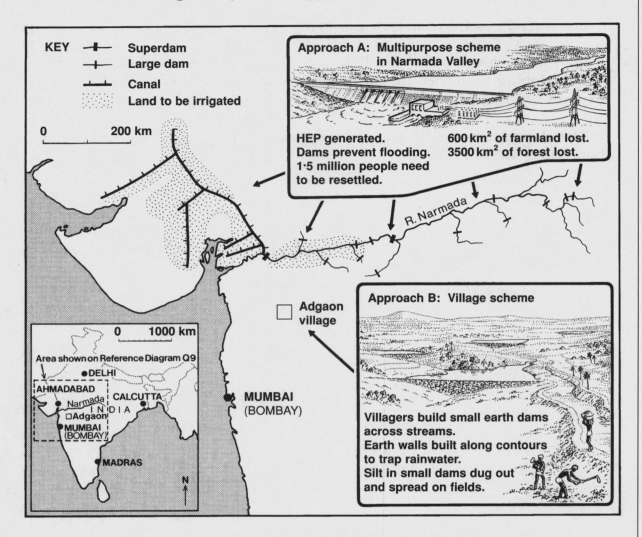

Look at Reference Diagram Q9 above.

The problem in this part of India is that there is a dry season and unpredictable rainfall.

Which approach, **A** or **B**, do you think is the more appropriate for a Developing Country such as India?

Give reasons for your answer.

Marks

KU | E

**10.**   **Reference Diagram Q10A: Possible Effects of giving Aid to Developing Countries**

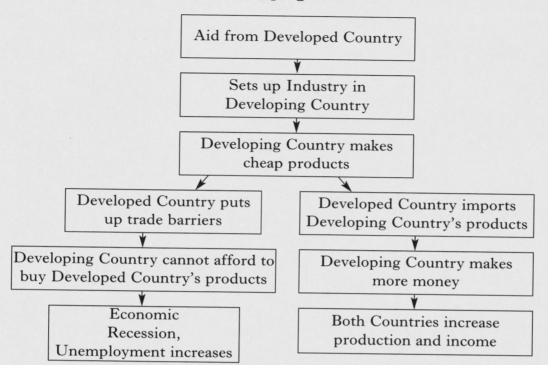

**Reference Diagram Q10B: Percentage of GNP spent on Aid by Developed Countries**

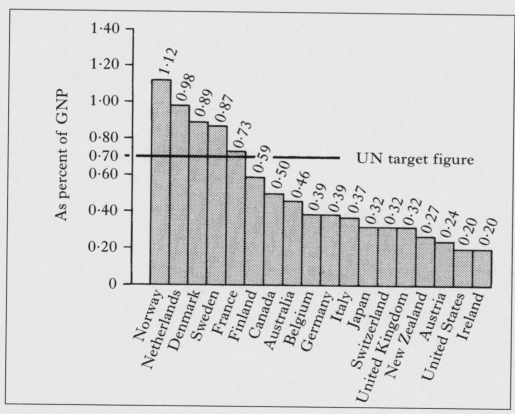

Look at Reference Diagrams Q10A and Q10B.

"Developed Countries are keen to give aid to Developing Countries because of the benefits involved."

Do you agree with this statement? Give reasons for your answer.

4

*[END OF QUESTION PAPER]*

[BLANK PAGE]

**C**

## 1260/405

NATIONAL
QUALIFICATIONS
2000

MONDAY, 5 JUNE
10.45 AM – 12.45 PM

**GEOGRAPHY**
STANDARD GRADE
Credit Level

All questions should be attempted.

Candidates should read the questions carefully. Answers should be clearly expressed and relevant.

Credit will always be given for appropriate sketch-maps and diagrams.

Write legibly and neatly, and leave a space of about one cm between the lines.

Marks may be deducted for bad spelling and bad punctuation, and for writing that is difficult to read.

All maps and diagrams in this paper have been printed in black only: no other colours have been used.

SCOTTISH
QUALIFICATIONS
AUTHORITY

©

1:50 000 Scale
Landranger Series

Four colours should appear above; if not then please return to the invigilator.
Four colours should appear above; if not then please return to the invigilator.

Extract No 1173/93

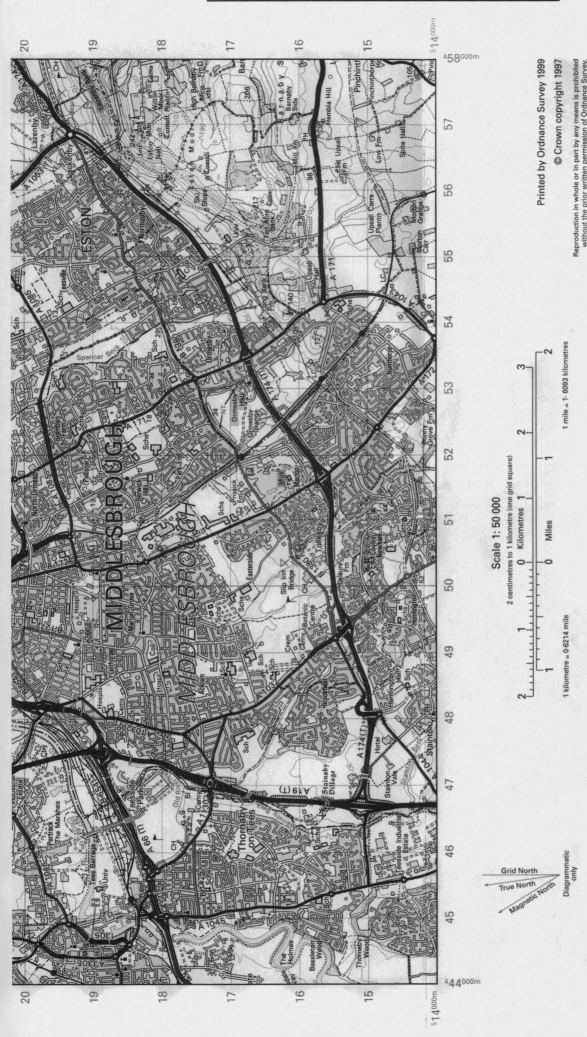

Scale 1: 50 000

2 centimetres to 1 kilometre (one grid square)

Kilometres

Miles

1 kilometre = 0·6214 mile

1 mile = 1· 6093 kilometres

Grid North

True North

Magnetic North

Diagrammatic
only

1.

**Reference Diagram Q1A**

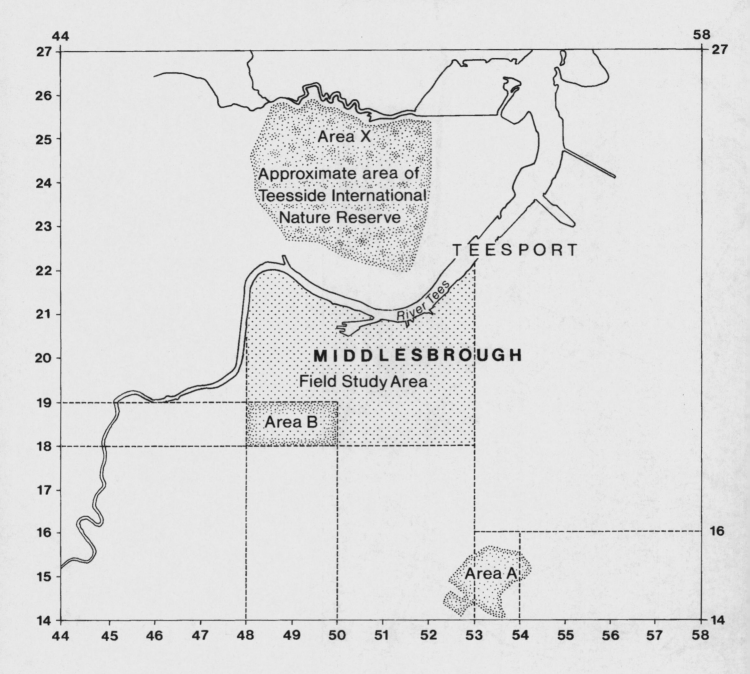

*Marks*

KU | E

## 1. (continued)

This question refers to the OS Map Extract (No 1173/93) of the Middlesbrough area and Reference Diagram Q1A.

(*a*) Give the four figure grid reference of the square which contains Middlesbrough's CBD (Central Business District). Give reasons for your answer.

3

(*b*) A group of students has been asked to gather information about urban and industrial change in the field study area marked on Reference Diagram Q1A.

Describe in detail the gathering techniques they might use to complete such an assignment. Justify your choices.

5

(*c*) Describe the differences between the two urban environments of Nunthorpe (Area A) and Linthorpe/Marton Grove (Area B), labelled on Reference Diagram Q1A.

5

(*d*) **Reference Diagram Q1B: Location of Middlesbrough/Teesport**

Teesport is one of Britain's largest ports and is the second largest petrochemicals port in Europe.

Using **map evidence** as well as Reference Diagram Q1B, **explain** the advantages of site and situation which Teesport has for manufacturing industries such as petrochemicals.

6

Marks
KU | E

## 1. (continued)

(e) Describe the **physical** features of the River Tees **and** its valley from Basselton Wood (446157) to the road bridge at (475194).

4

(f)     **Reference Text Q1C:  Teesside International Nature Reserve**

| Area: | 1000 hectares |
|---|---|
| Investment: | £11 million between 1998 and 2008 |
| Managed by: | Teesside Environment Trust |
| Proposal: | Creation of a massive open water, reedbed and swamp system.  Construction of a visitor centre, bird hides and a system of board walks through existing mudflats, salt marsh and open grassland. |
| Wildlife: | Includes endangered wading birds such as snipe, redshank, bittern and other migratory species. |

Look at Reference Text Q1C and Reference Diagram Q1A and locate Area X on the Ordnance Survey map.

Give the advantages **and** disadvantages of this site for a nature reserve.

2.　　　**Reference Diagram Q2:** **Weather Conditions over British Isles**
**October 1998**

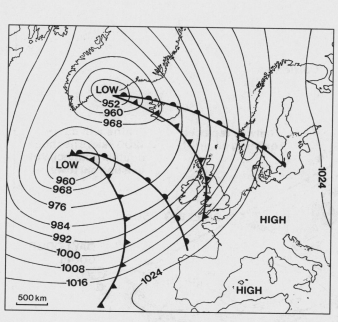

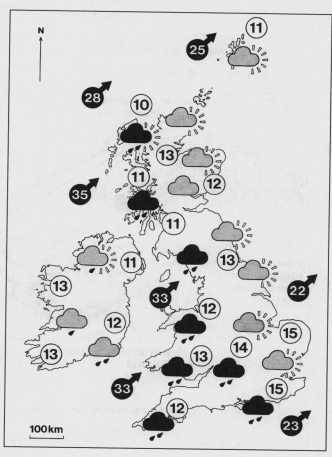

Look at Reference Diagram Q2.

**Explain** the differences in weather between the East and West of the British Isles.

Marks

| KU | E |
|---|---|
| 6 | |

**[Turn over**

**3.**     **Reference Diagram Q3A: The Cairn Gorm Mountain Railway**

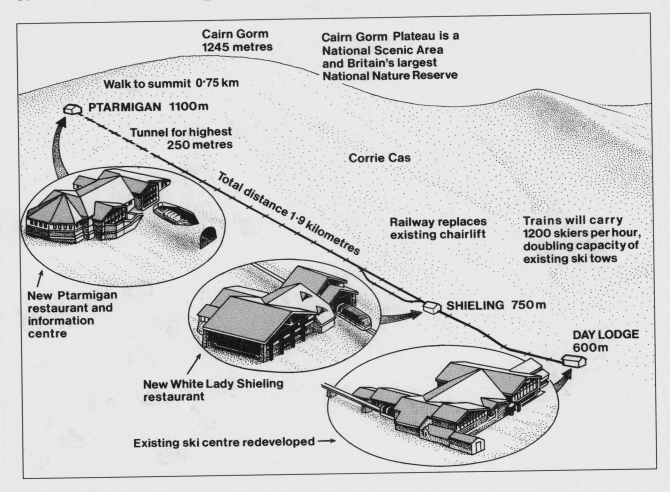

**Reference Diagram Q3B: Area around Aviemore and the Cairngorms**

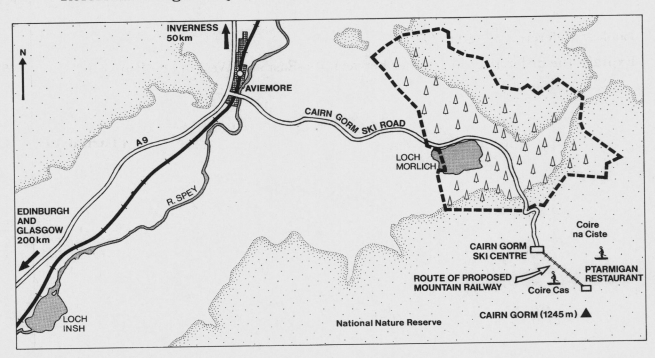

KEY    ▨ Land over 400 Metres    ⊏⊐ Glenmore Forest Park    ⚑ Ski slopes    Scale ⊢—⊣ 1 km

**3. (continued)**

### Reference Table Q3C: Selected Statistics for Aviemore and the Cairngorms

|  | With existing Ski Tows and Chairlifts | Estimated Figures after Opening of Mountain Railway |
|---|---|---|
| Cairn Gorm Ski Centre income | £3 million | £5 million |
| % of total income earned in winter months | 90 | 50 |
| People travelling up to Ptarmigan Restaurant in summer | 55 000 | 125 000 |
| People walking from Ptarmigan to Cairn Gorm summit in summer | 4400 | 12 500 |
| Tourist related jobs in Aviemore area | 600 | 960 |

*Marks*

| KU | ES |
|---|---|

(a) Study Reference Diagrams Q3A and Q3B and Reference Table Q3C.

"This development will be of tremendous benefit to the area."

Do you agree with this statement about the Cairn Gorm Mountain Railway? Give detailed reasons for your answer.

6

(b) University students will carry out a survey to assess the possible impact of the Cairn Gorm Mountain Railway on the area.

Which gathering techniques might they use to obtain appropriate data?

**Explain** in detail your choice of techniques.

5

**[Turn over**

*Marks*

KU | E

**4.** **Reference Text Q4A: Eire in the 1950s**

> In the 1950s, Eire was a country based on agriculture and characterised by emigration and a fairly low standard of living.

**Reference Diagram Q4B: Location of Eire in the EU**

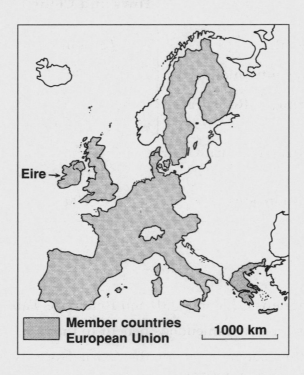

Eire →

■ Member countries
European Union

1000 km

**Reference Diagram Q4C: Eire in the late 1990s**

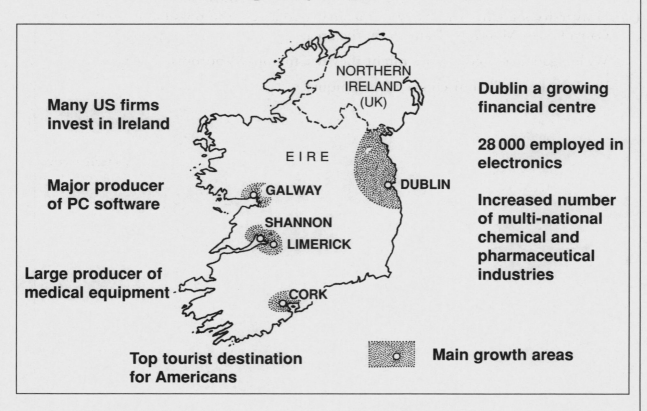

NORTHERN
IRELAND
(UK)

**Many US firms
invest in Ireland**

**Dublin a growing
financial centre**

EIRE

**28 000 employed in
electronics**

**Major producer
of PC software**

GALWAY

SHANNON

DUBLIN

**Increased number
of multi-national
chemical and
pharmaceutical
industries**

LIMERICK

**Large producer of
medical equipment**

CORK

**Top tourist destination
for Americans**

**Main growth areas**

**4. (continued)**

### Reference Text Q4D: Why firms are going to Eire

- Labour costs low by EU Standards

- Many university graduates

- Favourable tax system

- High quality environment

Study Reference Text Q4A, Reference Diagrams Q4B and Q4C and Reference Text Q4D.

"Over the last thirty years the economy of Eire has changed as many foreign firms have chosen to locate there."

Describe in detail the advantages **and** disadvantages which economic change has brought to Eire.

6

**[Turn over**

Marks

KU | E

5.    **Reference Diagram Q5:  Oil Industry in the Niger Delta (West Africa)**

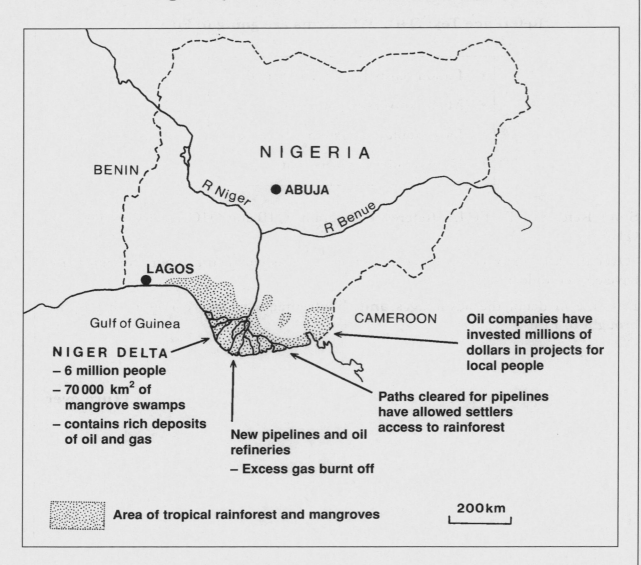

NIGERIA

BENIN

R Niger

● ABUJA

R Benue

LAGOS

Gulf of Guinea

CAMEROON

**Oil companies have invested millions of dollars in projects for local people**

**NIGER DELTA**
**– 6 million people**
**– 70 000 km² of mangrove swamps**
**– contains rich deposits of oil and gas**

**Paths cleared for pipelines have allowed settlers access to rainforest**

**New pipelines and oil refineries**
**– Excess gas burnt off**

**Area of tropical rainforest and mangroves**

200 km

**Reference Table Q5:  Facts about Oil in the Niger Delta**

| | |
|---|---|
| % of Nigeria's exports provided by oil | 90 |
| Number of oil spills in the Niger Delta (1976–1991) | 2976 |
| Number of people employed in the oil industry in Nigeria | 25 000 |

Study Reference Diagram Q5 and Reference Table Q5.

"The damage caused to the rainforest environment in the Niger Delta is a small price to pay for the huge benefits which the oil industry has brought to the people of the area."

Do you agree with this statement?  Give reasons for your answer.

*Marks*

KU | E

**6.** **Reference Diagram Q6A: Selected Statistics on International Debt**

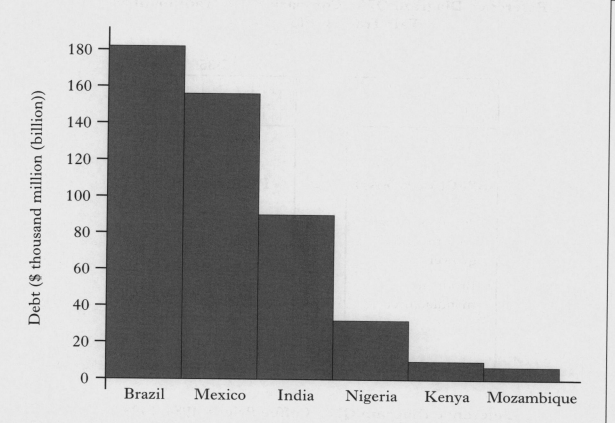

**Reference Text Q6B**

"Jubilee 2000 is encouraging Governments and International Banks to cancel the debts of many of the world's poorest countries."

Study Reference Diagram Q6A and Reference Text Q6B.

Explain how debt causes major problems for many developing countries.

4

**[Turn over**

**7.** **Reference Diagram Q7A: Comparison of Traditional and Fair Trade Coffee Prices**

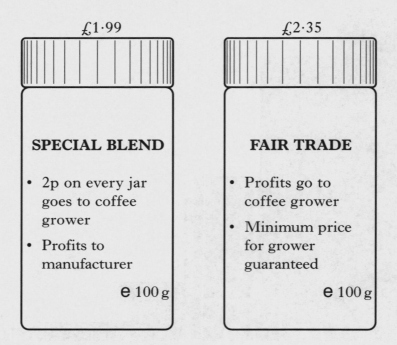

£1·99

**SPECIAL BLEND**

- 2p on every jar goes to coffee grower
- Profits to manufacturer

e 100 g

£2·35

**FAIR TRADE**

- Profits go to coffee grower
- Minimum price for grower guaranteed

e 100 g

**Reference Diagram Q7B: Coffee Prices, 1984–1998 (Coffee Beans)**

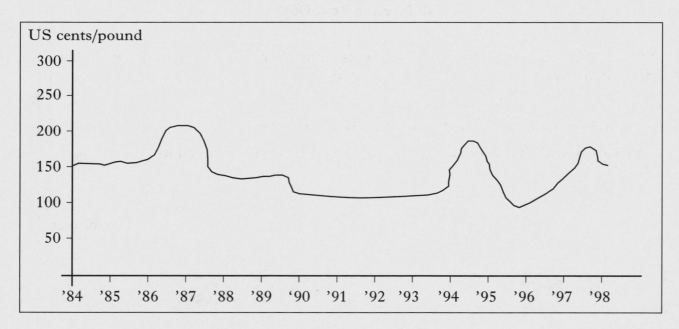

Marks
KU | E.

**7. (continued)**

**Reference Text Q7C: Extract from Fair Trade Advertisement**

---

**Perfect Coffee and How to Make It**

- Warm the pot, add one heaped spoon of freshly roasted Fair Trade coffee.
- Filter out the middleman.
- Provide coffee farmers with a regular income.
- Help turn mud and straw houses into bricks and mortar.
- Enjoy your coffee . . . and help build a brighter future for the next generation.
- A better deal guaranteed for coffee growers.

---

Look at Reference Diagrams Q7A and Q7B and Reference Text Q7C.

**Explain** how the idea of Fair Trade is a way of helping coffee growers in the Developing World.

4

**[Turn over**

*Marks*

KU

8. **Reference Table Q8: Selected Data for 5 Countries**

| | Land Area (sq km) | Population (million) | GDP ($/head) | Exports ($ million) | Imports ($ million) | Urban (percent) |
|---|---|---|---|---|---|---|
| USA | 9 100 000 | 255 | 22 470 | 428 | 499 | 75 |
| Brazil | 8 400 000 | 150 | 2300 | 31 | 21 | 74 |
| Japan | 374 000 | 124 | 19 000 | 314 | 236 | 77 |
| India | 2 900 000 | 882 | 380 | 20 | 25 | 25 |
| Russia | 17 000 000 | 149 | 2240 | 58 | 43 | 74 |

Look at Reference Table Q8.

(*a*) Suggest **two** methods you could use to show **relationships** between different data in the table. Justify your choices in detail.

(*b*) "Population size and land area are the main indicators which show the international importance of a country."

Do you agree with the above statement? Give reasons for your answer.

**9.**

## Reference Diagram Q9A: Population Density of Peru

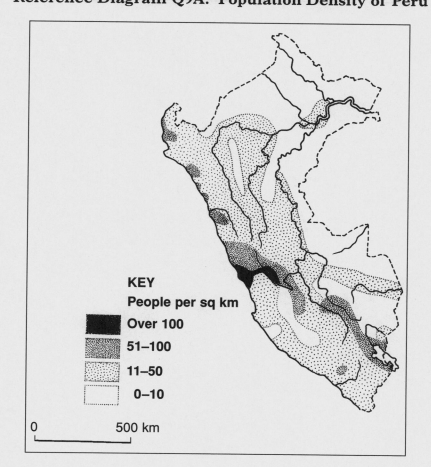

KEY

People per sq km

Over 100

51–100

11–50

0–10

0          500 km

**Reference Diagram Q9B:
Resources and Industry of Peru**

**Reference Diagram Q9C:
Physical Features of Peru**

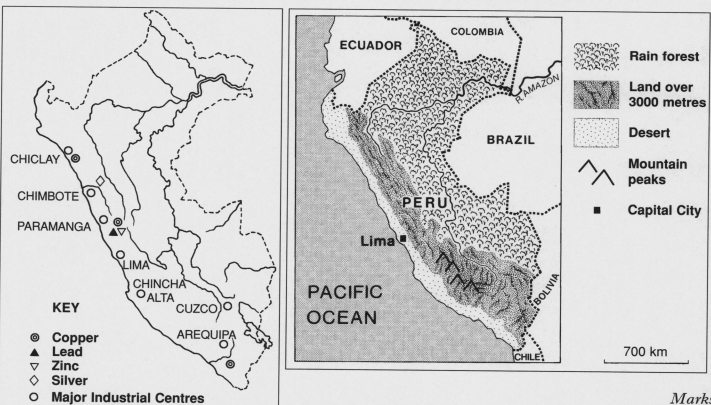

CHICLAY
CHIMBOTE
PARAMANGA
LIMA
CHINCHA
ALTA
CUZCO
AREQUIPA

KEY

◉ Copper
▲ Lead
▽ Zinc
◇ Silver
○ Major Industrial Centres

ECUADOR       COLOMBIA

R. AMAZON

BRAZIL

PERU

Lima

PACIFIC
OCEAN

BOLIVIA

CHILE

🌳 Rain forest

Land over
3000 metres

Desert

∧∧ Mountain
peaks

■ Capital City

700 km

Look at Reference Diagrams Q9A, Q9B and Q9C above.

**Explain** the population distribution of Peru.

*Marks*

| KU | ES |
|----|----|
| 4  |    |

[END OF QUESTION PAPER]

**[BLANK PAGE]**

C

# 1260/405

| | | |
|---|---|---|
| NATIONAL QUALIFICATIONS 2001 | WEDNESDAY, 23 MAY 10.45 AM – 12.45 PM | **GEOGRAPHY STANDARD GRADE** Credit Level |

All questions should be attempted.

Candidates should read the questions carefully. Answers should be clearly expressed and relevant.

Credit will always be given for appropriate sketch-maps and diagrams.

Write legibly and neatly, and leave a space of about one cm between the lines.

Marks may be deducted for bad spelling and bad punctuation, and for writing that is difficult to read.

All maps and diagrams in this paper have been printed in black only: no other colours have been used.

SCOTTISH QUALIFICATIONS AUTHORITY ©

Extract No 1213/19/24/25

1:50 000 Scale
Landranger Series

Four colours should appear above; if not then please return to the invigilator.
Four colours should appear above; if not then please return to the invigilator.

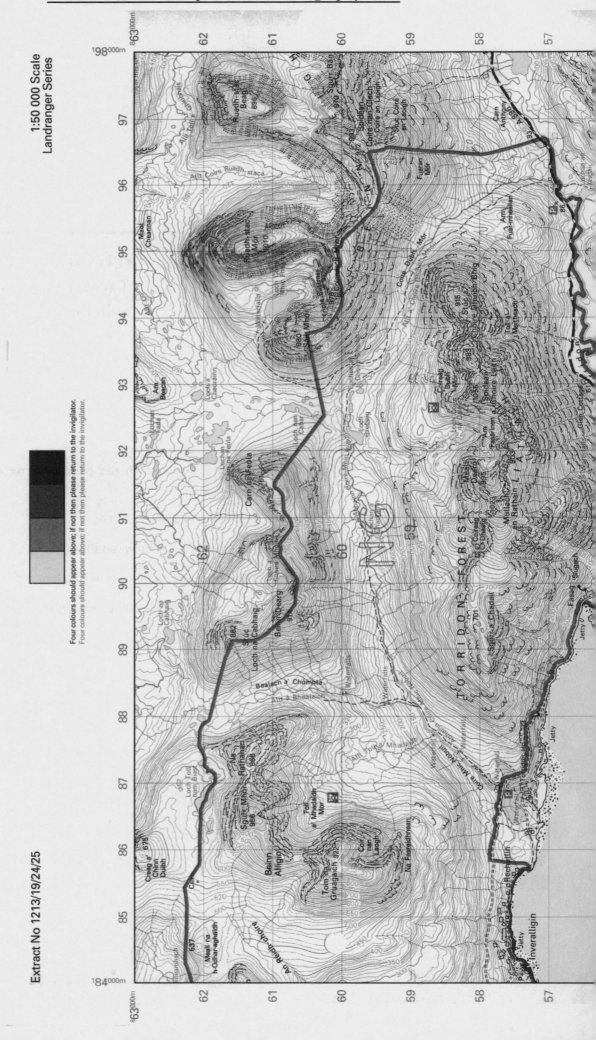

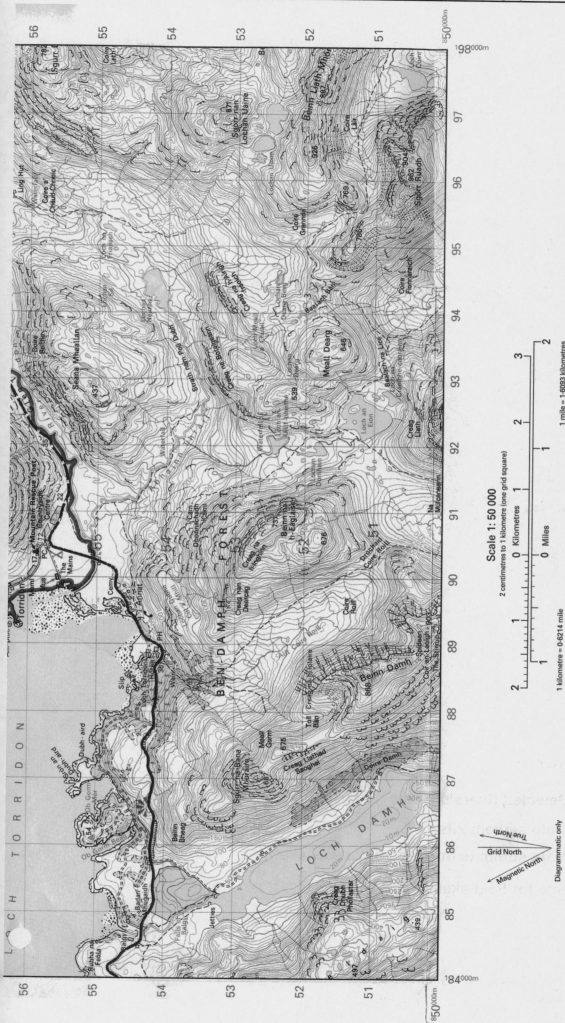

Scale 1:50 000

2 centimetres to 1 kilometre (one grid square)

1.

**Reference Diagram Q1A**

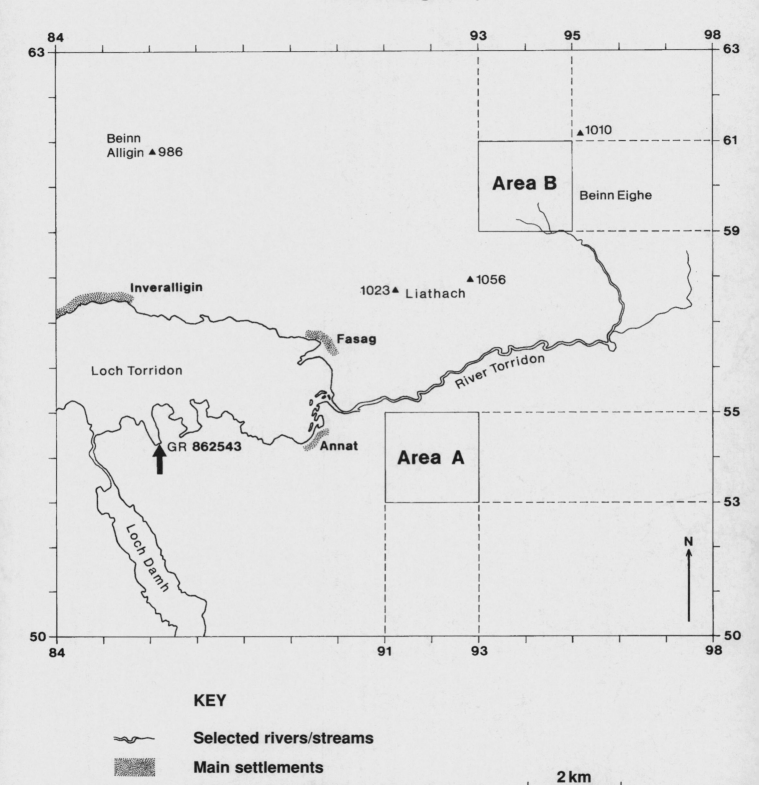

**KEY**

| | |
|---|---|
| ~~~ | **Selected rivers/streams** |
| ▓ | **Main settlements** |
| ▲1056 | **Main summits (metres above sea level)** |
| ⬆ | **Site for field sketch** |

2 km

*Marks*

KU    E

## 1. (continued)

This question refers to the OS Map Extract (No 1213/19/24/25) of Torridon and Reference Diagram Q1A on *Page two*.

(*a*) The area covered by the map extract is one of Scotland's most spectacular mountain landscapes.

  (i) Match each of the features named below with the correct grid reference.

  Features: pyramidal peak,    hanging valley,    arete,    corrie

  Choose from:

  Grid references: 952588,    923580,    852585,    860601,    925576    **3**

  (ii) **Explain** how **one** of the features listed in (*a*)(i) was formed.  You may use diagrams to illustrate your answer.    **4**

(*b*) Look at Reference Diagram Q1A.

A commercial forestry company surveyed the map area's potential for forestry.  It considered Area A to be more suitable than Area B.

Using map evidence, suggest **three** reasons for this.    **3**

### Reference Diagram Q1B:  A Hydro-electric Power Scheme

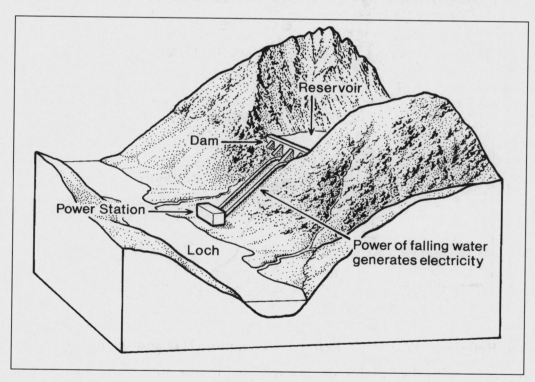

(*c*) Look at Reference Diagram Q1B.

There is a plan to construct a similar dam and power station in grid square 8853.

Using map evidence, describe the advantages **and** disadvantages of building such a scheme at this site.    **6**

## 1. (continued)

### Reference Text Q1C:  Report of Economic Survey

"Torridon is an ideal place for a large scale tourist development.   The benefits to the area would outweigh the disadvantages."

### Reference Diagram Q1D:  The Location of Torridon

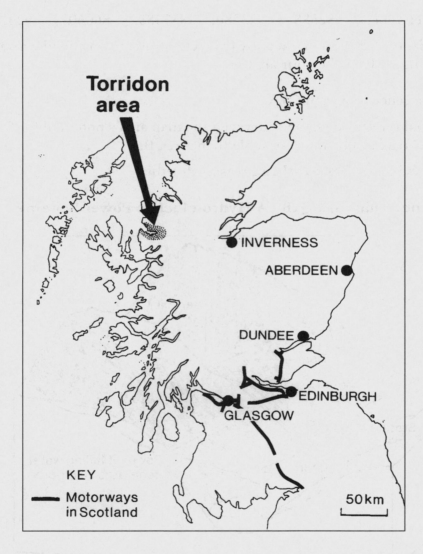

(d)  Look at Reference Text Q1C, Reference Diagram Q1D and the map extract.

Do you agree with the opinion being expressed by the authors of the report?

Making reference to map evidence, give reasons for your answer.

**1. (continued)**

**Reference Diagram Q1E:  Field Sketch looking North to Ben Alligin from GR 862543**

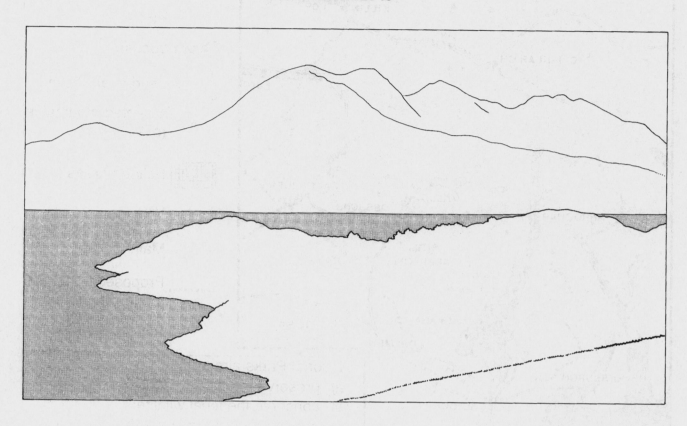

(e)  A student has gathered information for a physical landscape investigation.

The information includes the outline field sketch shown above in Reference Diagram Q1E, a photograph of the same view, a geology map and the OS map extract.

What techniques should the student now use to **process** this information?

Justify your choices.

4

**[Turn over**

**2.** **Reference Diagram Q2A: Loch Lomond and the Trossachs**

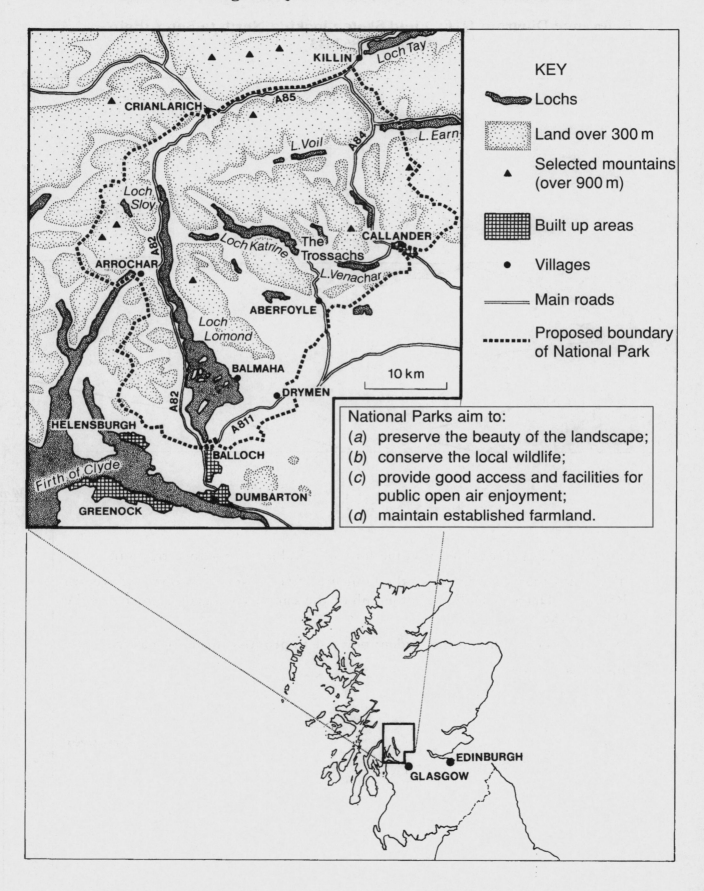

KEY

Lochs

Land over 300 m

Selected mountains (over 900 m)

Built up areas

Villages

Main roads

Proposed boundary of National Park

10 km

National Parks aim to:
(a) preserve the beauty of the landscape;
(b) conserve the local wildlife;
(c) provide good access and facilities for public open air enjoyment;
(d) maintain established farmland.

**2. (continued)**

**Reference Diagram Q2B: Land Users in the Loch Lomond and Trossachs Area**

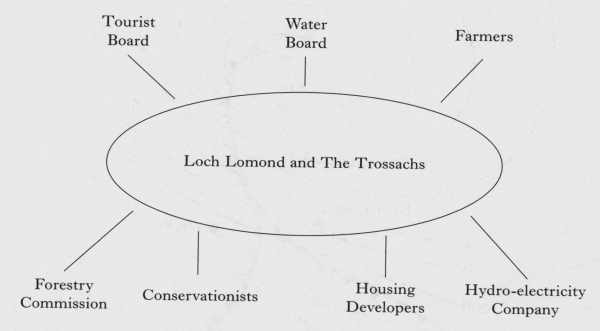

Study Reference Diagrams Q2A and Q2B.

Loch Lomond and The Trossachs was chosen as Scotland's first National Park.

Do you think all land users in Reference Diagram Q2B will welcome the establishment of this National Park?

**Explain** your answer.

6

**[Turn over**

*Marks*

KU E

3.    **Reference Diagram Q3: Synoptic Chart for British Isles
at 0700 hours on 31 August**

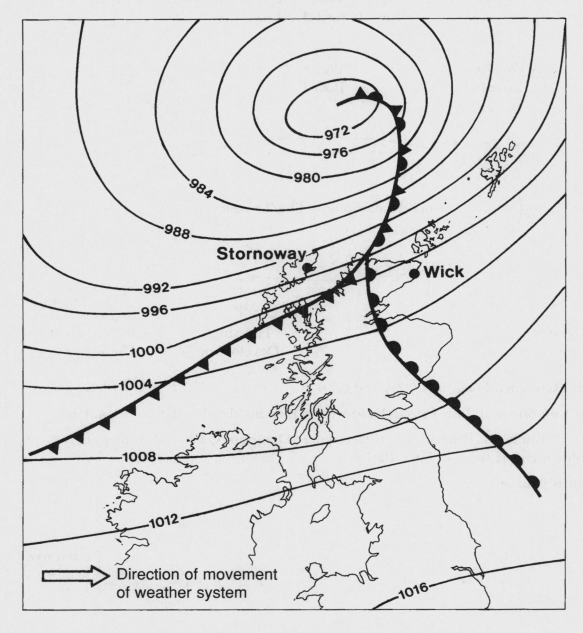

Look at Reference Diagram Q3.

A yacht race from Wick to Stornoway was due to start from Wick harbour at 8.00 am on 31 August.

At 7.00 am the Meteorological (Met) Office advised the race organisers to cancel the race.

With reference to the synoptic chart, **explain** why this advice was given.

5

**4. Reference Diagram Q4A: Urban Transect along Queen's Road, Aberdeen**

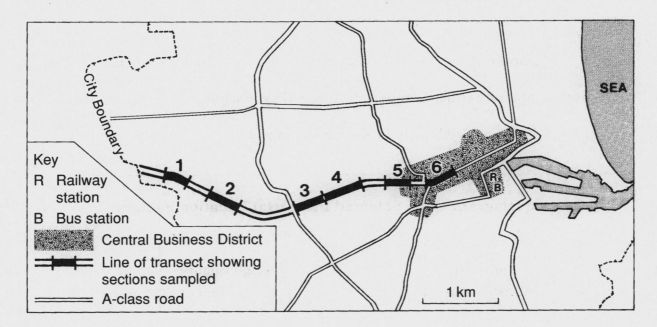

**Reference Diagram Q4B: Data collected along Transect**

| Sample point | 1 | 2 | 3 | 4 | 5 | 6 |
|---|---|---|---|---|---|---|
| Building height (storeys) | 2 | 2 | 3 | 4 | 4 | 4 |
| Number of Pedestrians | 2 | 4 | 7 | 8 | 17 | 64 |

Look at Reference Diagrams Q4A and Q4B.

(a) What techniques could have been used to gather the information in Reference Diagram Q4B?

Give reasons for your choices.

**6**

(b) **Explain** the changes that occur along the transect from the edge of the city to the centre.

**6**

**5.**  **Reference Diagram Q5A: Examples of High-Technology Industry**

Computers                    Lasers                    Body scanners

Semiconductors (silicon chips)            Fax machines

Satellite and rocket components

**Reference Diagram Q5B: Selected Industrial Location Factors**

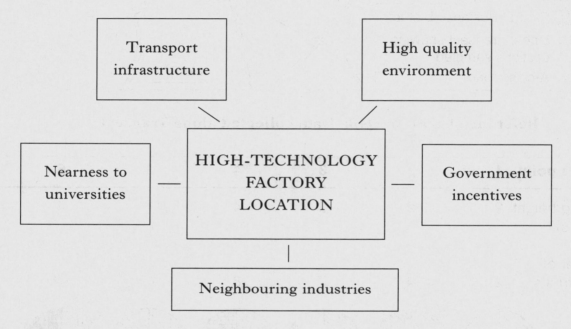

Study Reference Diagrams Q5A and Q5B.

**Explain** in what ways the factors listed above are important in the location of high-technology industries.

5

**6.**

**Reference Diagram Q6:  Births per Woman and Infant Mortality in Selected Countries**

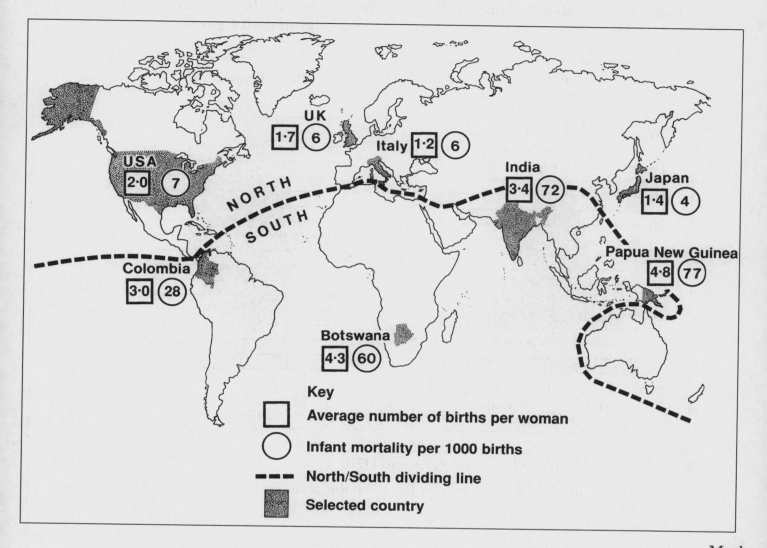

**Key**

☐ **Average number of births per woman**

◯ **Infant mortality per 1000 births**

– – – **North/South dividing line**

▓ **Selected country**

|  | Marks | |
| --- | --- | --- |
|  | KU | ES |

(a)  Look at Reference Diagram Q6.

Describe the patterns of births per woman and infant mortality, as shown in Reference Diagram Q6. | | **4**

(b)  Explain the differences in the patterns between North and South. | **3** |

(c)  What measures have **developing** nations taken to reduce population growth **and** infant mortality rates? | **4** |

[Turn over

**7.** **Reference Diagram Q7A:** **Reference Diagram Q7B:**
**Japan's Population Pyramid 1950** **Japan's Population Pyramid 2050**
**(projected figures)**

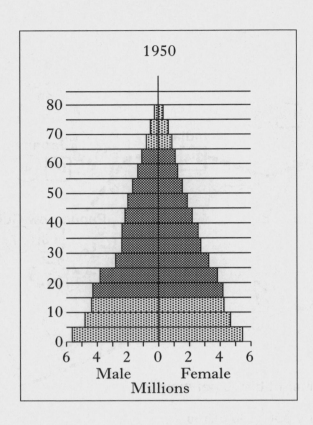

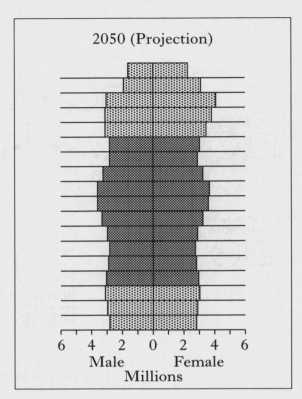

(a) Look at Reference Diagrams Q7A and Q7B.

Describe in detail the changes in Japan's population structure between 1950 and 2050.

(b) Do you agree that the changes in population structure will cause problems for the Japanese government by 2050?

State yes **or** no, and give reasons for your answer.

Marks

KU    E

**8.**

### Reference Table Q8A:  Kenya—Exports and Imports

| Exports | % | Imports | % |
|---|---|---|---|
| Foodstuffs | 59 | Manufactured goods | 40 |
| Minerals and fuels | 21 | Minerals and fuels | 23 |
| Machinery and transport | 9 | Machinery and transport | 13 |
| Chemicals | 4 | Chemicals | 11 |
| Manufactured goods | 3 | Foodstuffs | 9 |
| Others | 4 | Others | 4 |
| Total ($ million) | $1028 | Total ($ million) | $2136 |

### Reference Table Q8B:  Kenya—Direction of Trade

| Trading Partners | % of Exports | % of Imports |
|---|---|---|
| European Union | 43 | 43 |
| (including UK) | (16) | (16) |
| African countries | 18 | 2 |
| United Arab Emirates | — | 12 |
| Japan | 3 | 12 |
| USA | 4 | 4 |
| Others | 32 | 27 |

(a) Look at Reference Tables Q8A and Q8B.

Describe the pattern of Kenya's trade.

4

(b) Describe methods you could use to process the information shown in Reference Tables Q8A and Q8B.

Justify your choices.

6

*[END OF QUESTION PAPER]*

**[BLANK PAGE]**

**C**

# 1260/405

NATIONAL
QUALIFICATIONS
2002

MONDAY, 13 MAY
1.00 PM – 3.00 PM

GEOGRAPHY
STANDARD GRADE
Credit Level

All questions should be attempted.

Candidates should read the questions carefully. Answers should be clearly expressed and relevant.

Credit will always be given for appropriate sketch-maps and diagrams.

Write legibly and neatly, and leave a space of about one cm between the lines.

Marks may be deducted for bad spelling and bad punctuation, and for writing that is difficult to read.

All maps and diagrams in this paper have been printed in black only: no other colours have been used.

SCOTTISH
QUALIFICATIONS
AUTHORITY

©

1:50 000 Scale
Landranger Series

Extract No 1267/38

Four colours should appear above; if not then please return to the invigilator.
Four colours should appear above; if not then please return to the invigilator.

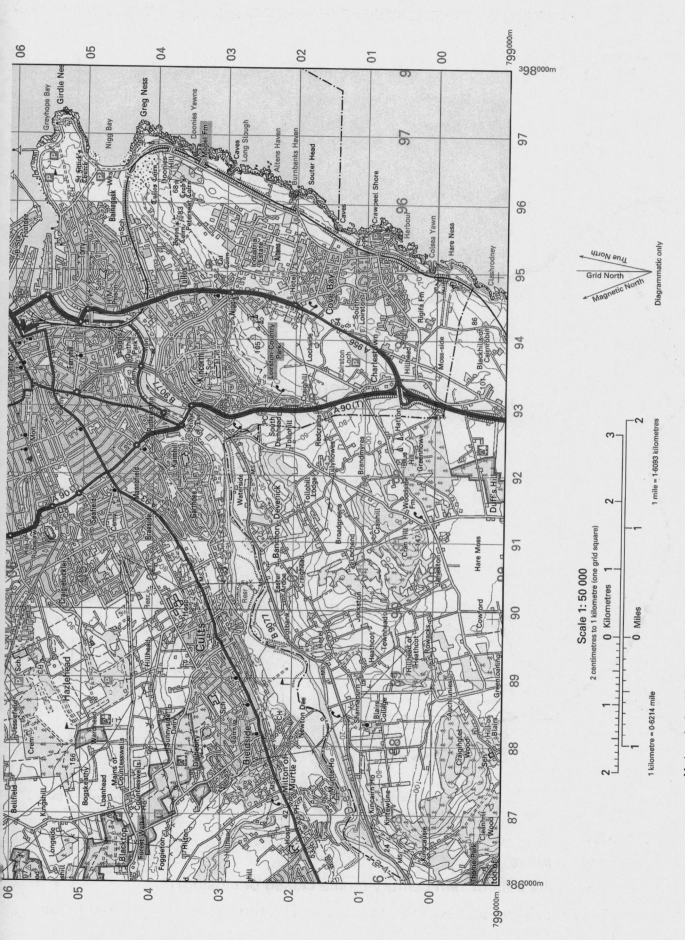

Scale 1: 50 000

2 centimetres to 1 kilometre (one grid square)

Made and printed by Ordnance Survey 2001
© Crown copyright 1999

Ordnance Survey, the OS Symbol and Landranger are registered trademarks of Ordnance Survey, the national mapping agency of Great Britain.
Reproduction in whole or in part by any means is prohibited without the prior written permission of Ordnance Survey. **For educational use only.**

**1.**

**Reference Diagram Q1A**

**KEY**

| | |
|---|---|
| Built up areas | |
| **1** Paper mills built in 19th century (some closed or closing) | |
| **2** Fish processing and services to offshore oil industry | **Industrial Areas** |
| **3** Modern industrial estate | |

Marks

KU | ES

**1. (continued)**

This question refers to the OS Map Extract (No 1267/38) of Aberdeen and Reference Diagram Q1A on *Page two*.

(a) Look at Reference Diagram Q1A, showing the proposed route of a major new road.

Do you think this road should be built?

Use map evidence to justify your answer.

6

**Reference Diagram Q1B: Model of Urban Land Use**

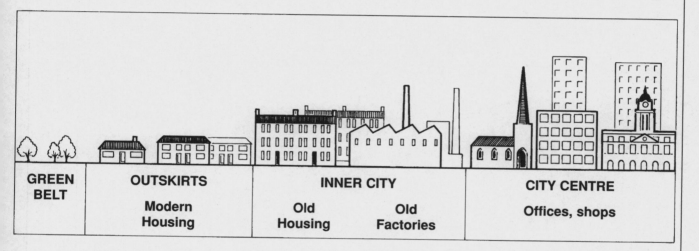

(b) Look at Reference Diagram Q1B above which shows a model of land use from the centre to the edge of a city.

Look at the OS map extract. Find the transect drawn from A (865070) to B (960057) on Reference Diagram Q1A.

Describe the similarities **and** differences in land use between the model and those found along transect AB.

6

(c) **Explain** the locations of the different industrial zones numbered **1**, **2** and **3** on Reference Diagram Q1A.

6

**[Turn over**

*Marks*

KU

## 1. (continued)

(*d*) Study the course of the River Dee and its valley between 866010 and 929035. Describe how the **physical** features of the river and its valley have influenced land use.

(*e*) Air transport is increasingly important to the economy of cities such as Aberdeen.

Look at Aberdeen Airport shown on Reference Diagram Q1A and the Ordnance Survey Map extract.

Using map evidence, describe the advantages **and** disadvantages of the site of Aberdeen Airport.

2. **Reference Diagram Q2: A Corrie in the Scottish Highlands**

Look at Reference Diagram Q2.

**Explain** the formation of a corrie. You may use diagram(s) to illustrate your answer.    4

**[Turn over**

3.  **Reference Diagram Q3: Synoptic Chart for British Isles,
    Sunday 10 December 2000**

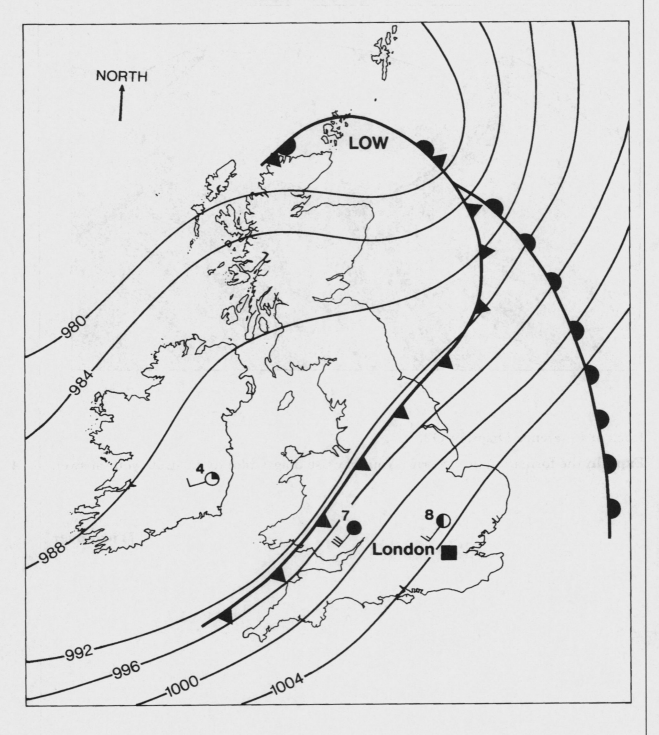

*Marks*

| KU | E |
|----|---|

## 3. (continued)

Look at Reference Diagram Q3.

(*a*) Describe in detail the weather conditions being experienced in London on Sunday 10 December 2000.

4

(*b*) "There will be some heavy showers of rain, giving way to sunny intervals. Winds, at first strong, will become lighter. Temperatures will drop."

(Forecast for London for Monday 11 December)

Give reasons for the changes which the weather forecasters believe will take place in London on Monday 11 December.

4

**[Turn over**

**4.**  **Reference Diagram Q4A:  Burgar Hill**

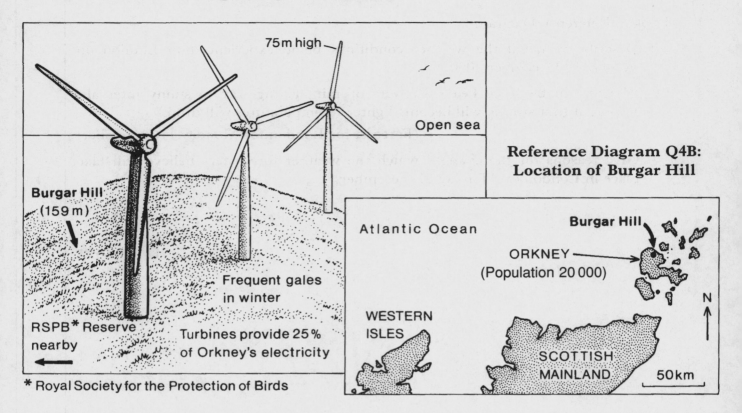

75 m high

Open sea

**Reference Diagram Q4B:
Location of Burgar Hill**

Burgar Hill
(159 m)

RSPB* Reserve
nearby

Frequent gales
in winter

Turbines provide 25 %
of Orkney's electricity

* Royal Society for the Protection of Birds

Atlantic Ocean

Burgar Hill

ORKNEY
(Population 20 000)

WESTERN
ISLES

SCOTTISH
MAINLAND

N

50 km

*Marks*

| KU | E |

Look at Reference Diagrams Q4A and Q4B.

Three large wind turbines have been constructed on Burgar Hill in Orkney.

What are the advantages **and** disadvantages of having wind turbines in this area?

*Marks*
KU | E

**5.** **Reference Diagram Q5: Sphere of Influence of Inverness**

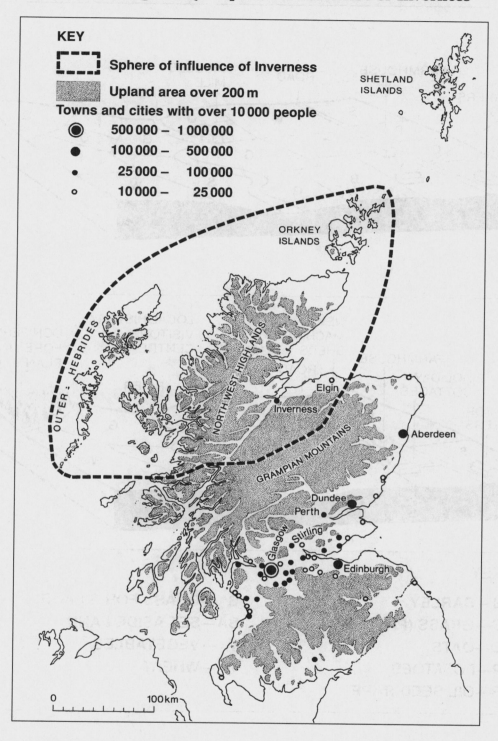

**KEY**

- - - Sphere of influence of Inverness

▒ Upland area over 200 m

**Towns and cities with over 10 000 people**

◉ 500 000 – 1 000 000
● 100 000 – 500 000
• 25 000 – 100 000
○ 10 000 – 25 000

SHETLAND ISLANDS

ORKNEY ISLANDS

OUTER HEBRIDES

NORTH WEST HIGHLANDS

Elgin
Inverness

Aberdeen

GRAMPIAN MOUNTAINS

Dundee
Perth

Glasgow
Stirling

Edinburgh

0        100km

(a) Describe the gathering techniques which could have been used to identify the sphere of influence of Inverness as shown in Reference Diagram Q5.

Justify your choice of techniques.

6

(b) Look at Reference Diagram Q5.

The sphere of influence of Inverness has an unusual size and shape.

Suggest reasons for this.

4

**6.**

### Reference Diagram Q6A: Changing Land Use on Clook Farm

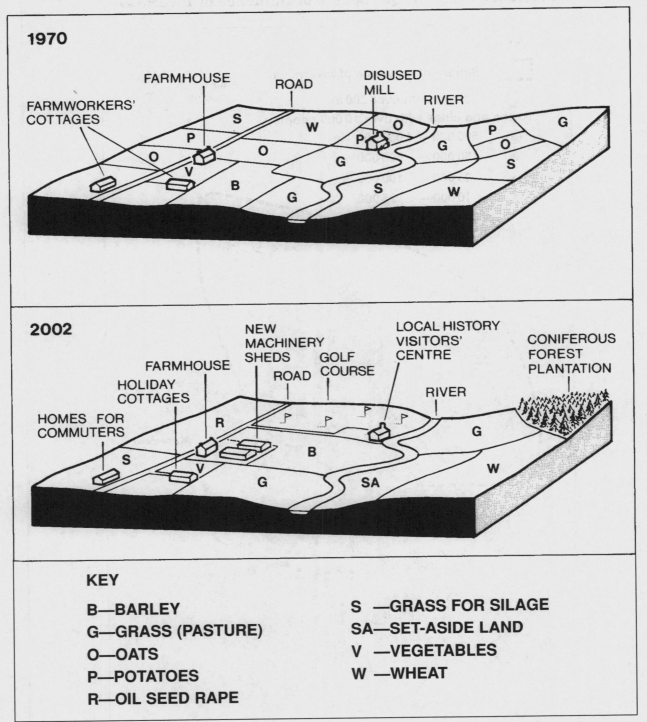

**1970**

FARMWORKERS' COTTAGES

FARMHOUSE

ROAD

DISUSED MILL

RIVER

**2002**

HOMES FOR COMMUTERS

HOLIDAY COTTAGES

FARMHOUSE

NEW MACHINERY SHEDS

ROAD

GOLF COURSE

LOCAL HISTORY VISITORS' CENTRE

RIVER

CONIFEROUS FOREST PLANTATION

**KEY**

**B—BARLEY**

**G—GRASS (PASTURE)**

**O—OATS**

**P—POTATOES**

**R—OIL SEED RAPE**

**S —GRASS FOR SILAGE**

**SA—SET-ASIDE LAND**

**V —VEGETABLES**

**W —WHEAT**

*Marks*

| KU | ES |
|----|----|

(*a*) Give reasons for the changes in land use on Clook Farm between 1970 and the present day.

**6**

**6. (continued)**

**Reference Table Q6B: Percentage Land Use on Clook Farm**

|  | 1970 | 2002 |
|---|---|---|
| Barley | 10 | 15 |
| Grass (pasture) | 25 | 28 |
| Oats | 15 | 0 |
| Potatoes | 10 | 0 |
| Oil seed rape | 0 | 10 |
| Grass for silage | 15 | 12 |
| Set aside land | 0 | 10 |
| Vegetables | 10 | 5 |
| Wheat | 15 | 8 |
| Golf course | 0 | 7 |
| Forestry | 0 | 5 |

(b) Study Reference Table Q6B.

Suggest **two** other processing techniques which could be used to show this information. Give reasons for your choices.

5

**[Turn over**

*Marks*

KU | E

7.

### Reference Diagram Q7A:
### Population Density of South Island, New Zealand

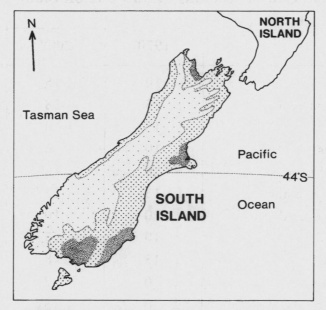

Over 20 persons per square kilometre

2 to 20 persons per square kilometre

0 to 1 person per square kilometre

### Reference Diagram Q7B:
### Relief and Physical Resources

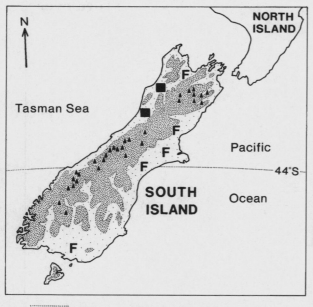

Peaks over 2000 metres

Land over 400 metres
(The Southern Alps)

Land under 400 metres

F   Best farmland

Coalfields

### Reference Diagram Q7C:
### Annual Rainfall

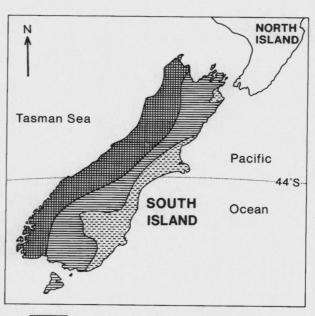

Over 1700 mm per year

700 to 1700 mm per year

Less than 700 mm per year

0      500 km

*Marks*

KU | E

**7. (continued)**

(*a*)  Look at Reference Diagrams Q7A, Q7B and Q7C.

**Explain** the population distribution on South Island, New Zealand.

4

**[Turn over**

Marks

KU ES

## 7. (continued)

**Reference Diagram Q7D: Population Pyramids for New Zealand and Indonesia**

(b) Look at Reference Diagram Q7D.

"New Zealand is a developed country and Indonesia is a developing country."

Give reasons for the differences between the population structures of New Zealand and Indonesia.

6

8.                    **Reference Diagram Q8:  World Trade**

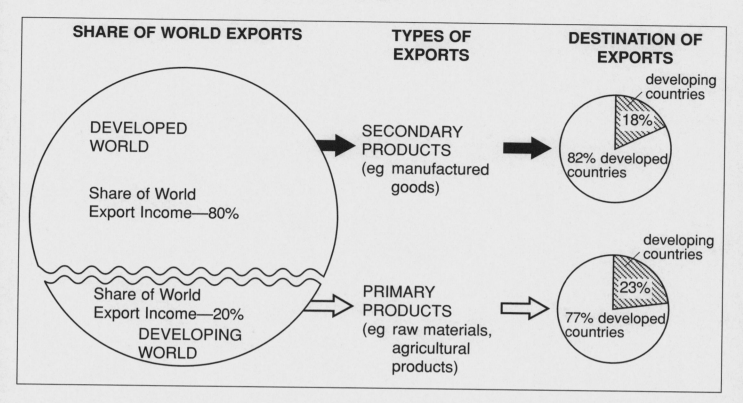

"The pattern of world trade benefits only countries of the Developed World."

Do you agree with this statement?

Give reasons for your answer.

Marks

| KU | ES |
|----|----|
|    | 5  |

[END OF QUESTION PAPER]

**[BLANK PAGE]**

2003 CREDIT

**C**

# 1260/405

NATIONAL
QUALIFICATIONS
2003

THURSDAY, 15 MAY
1.00 PM – 3.00 PM

GEOGRAPHY
STANDARD GRADE
Credit Level

All questions should be attempted.

Candidates should read the questions carefully. Answers should be clearly expressed and relevant.

Credit will always be given for appropriate sketch-maps and diagrams.

Write legibly and neatly, and leave a space of about one cm between the lines.

Marks may be deducted for bad spelling and bad punctuation, and for writing that is difficult to read.

All maps and diagrams in this paper have been printed in black only: no other colours have been used.

SCOTTISH
QUALIFICATIONS
AUTHORITY
©

Extract No 1323/36/43

1:50 000 Scale
Landranger Series

Four colours should appear above; if not then please return to the invigilator.
Four colours should appear above; if not then please return to the invigilator.

BEINN A BHUIRD

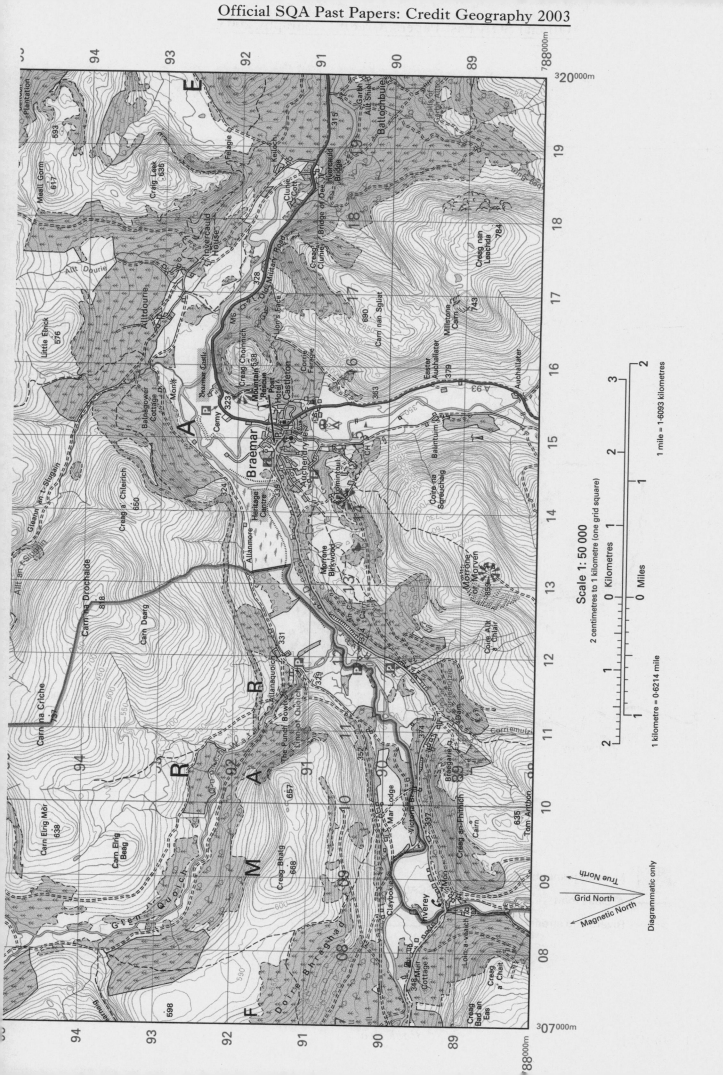

**1.**

## Reference Diagram Q1A

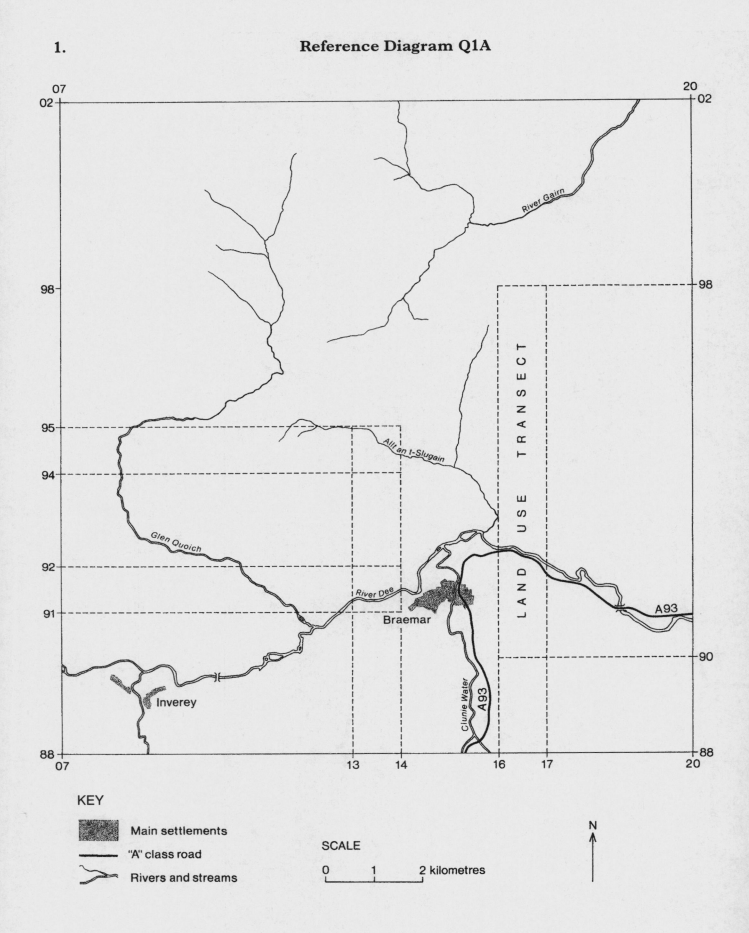

**KEY**

Main settlements

"A" class road

Rivers and streams

SCALE

0    1    2 kilometres

N

Marks
KU  E

**1. (continued)**

This question refers to the OS Map Extract (No 1323/36/43) of the Braemar Area and the Reference Diagram Q1A on *Page two.*

(*a*)  (i)  Match each of the features named below with the correct grid reference.

Features:  hanging valley;  truncated spur;  corrie;  U shaped valley.

Choose from grid references:  094992,  134996,  155993,  146980.      3

(ii)  **Explain** how **one** of these features listed in (*a*)(i) was formed.

You may use diagrams to illustrate your answer.      4

**Reference Diagram Q1B:  Requirements for National Park Status**

| | |
|---|---|
| *High quality landscape* | *Variety of plant and animal habitats* |
| *Recreation and tourist value* | *Historic features* |

**Reference Diagram Q1C:  Main Land Uses in the Braemar Area**

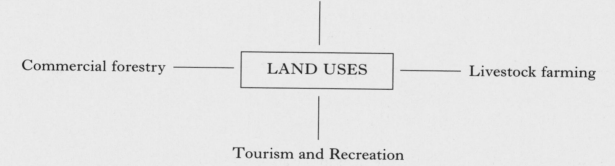

Grouse shooting and deer stalking

Commercial forestry —————— LAND USES —————— Livestock farming

Tourism and Recreation

(*b*)  Look at Reference Diagrams Q1B and Q1C.

The whole of the area covered by the OS map extract is within the recently designated Cairngorm National Park.

Describe the advantages **and** disadvantages this area has for a national park.

Use map evidence to support your answer.      6

**[Turn over**

*Marks*

KU ES

## 1. (continued)

(*c*) Study Reference Diagram Q1A and the OS map extract.

The Rivers Dee (1391) and Allt an t-Slugain (1394) and their valleys are very different.

Describe these differences **in detail**.

4

**Reference Diagram Q1D:  Settlement Pattern around Braemar**

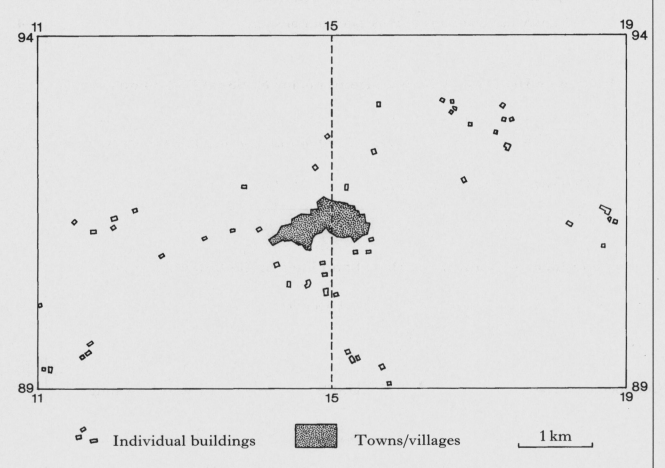

Individual buildings          Towns/villages          1 km

(*d*) **Explain** the distribution of settlement in the area of the map extract as shown by Reference Diagram Q1D.

6

Marks

KU | E

**1. (continued)**

### Reference Diagram Q1E: Land Use Transect

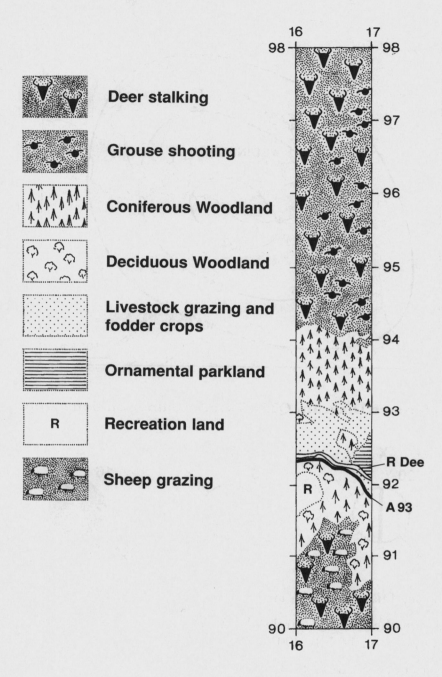

Deer stalking

Grouse shooting

Coniferous Woodland

Deciduous Woodland

Livestock grazing and fodder crops

Ornamental parkland

R    Recreation land

Sheep grazing

(e) Look at Reference Diagram Q1E, Reference Diagram Q1A and the OS map.

Give reasons for the pattern of land use which is shown on the transect.

**6**

**[Turn over**

Marks

KU | E

**2. Reference Diagram Q2A: European Synoptic Chart for Noon, 14 July 2001**

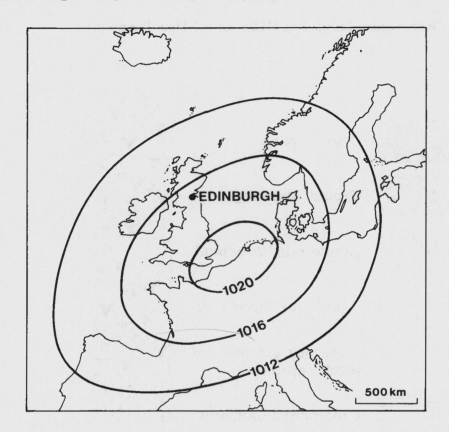

**Reference Diagram Q2B: Three Weather Station Circles**

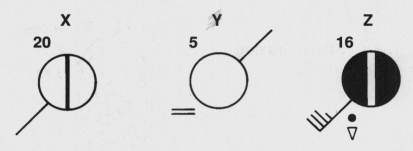

Study Reference Diagrams Q2A and Q2B.

State which weather station circle (**X**, **Y** or **Z**) shows the weather conditions at Edinburgh at noon on 14 July 2001.

**Explain** your choice **in detail**.

5

X

The wind is coming from the south West because there is an anti-cyclone. This area of high pressure brings dry calm weather with very little cloud cover.

Y cannot be the forecast as the wind is coming from the wrong direction.

X cannot be the forecast as there are rain showers expected & there is a lot of cloud cover.

*Page six*

3.     **Reference Diagram Q3:  Changing Landscape in West Africa**

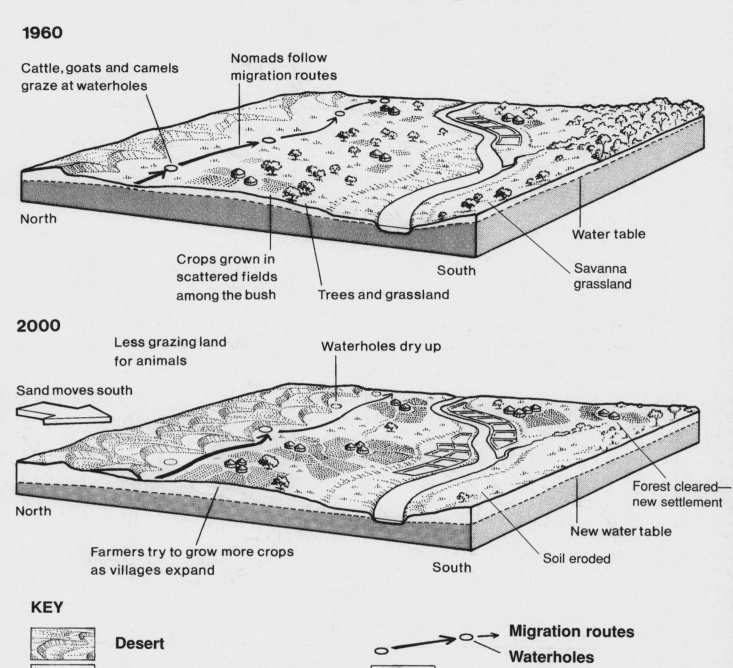

**1960**

Cattle, goats and camels graze at waterholes

Nomads follow migration routes

North

Crops grown in scattered fields among the bush

Trees and grassland

South

Water table

Savanna grassland

**2000**

Less grazing land for animals

Waterholes dry up

Sand moves south

North

Farmers try to grow more crops as villages expand

South

Forest cleared— new settlement

New water table

Soil eroded

**KEY**

Desert

Bush (trees/grassland)

Tropical forest

Migration routes

Waterholes

Irrigated crop land

Other crop land

Look at Reference Diagram Q3.

Give reasons for the changes in the landscapes of West Africa.

*Marks*

KU | ES

6

**4.** **Reference Diagram Q4A: Site of Shrewsbury**

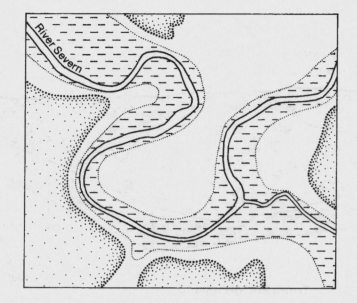

**KEY**

 Flood plain

 Land over 60 m

1 km

**Reference Diagram Q4B:**
**Shrewsbury in 16th century**

**Reference Diagram Q4C:**
**Shrewsbury in 2000**

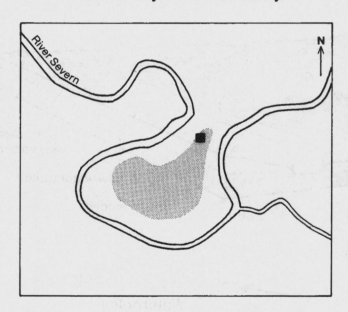

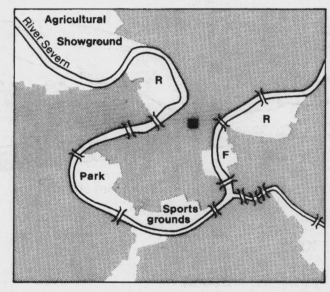

**KEY**

☐ **Open space**   ■ **Castle**   R **Recreation fields**

▨ **Built up area**   ⋈ **Bridge**   F **Football grounds**

*Marks*

| KU | ES |
|----|----|

Look at Reference Diagrams Q4A, Q4B and Q4C.

**Explain** the ways in which the River Severn has influenced Shrewsbury in terms of its site, growth and land use.

6

**5.**  **Reference Diagram Q5:  Sketch of Keilor Farm**

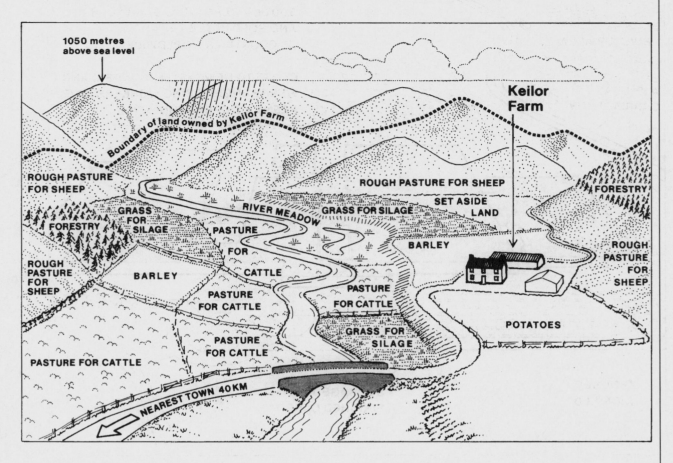

Study Reference Diagram Q5.

Keilor farm is a hill farm producing mainly beef cattle and sheep.

**Explain** the links between land use and the physical and human factors affecting the farm.

6

**[Turn over**

**6. Reference Diagram Q6A: Nissan Car Factory, Washington (View looking South)**

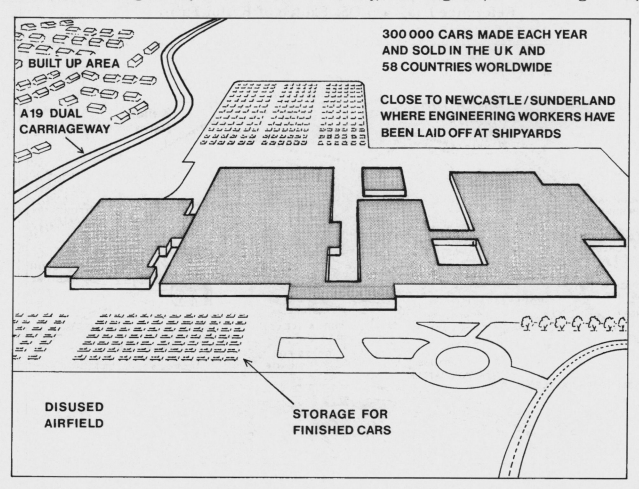

BUILT UP AREA

A19 DUAL
CARRIAGEWAY

300 000 CARS MADE EACH YEAR
AND SOLD IN THE UK AND
58 COUNTRIES WORLDWIDE

CLOSE TO NEWCASTLE / SUNDERLAND
WHERE ENGINEERING WORKERS HAVE
BEEN LAID OFF AT SHIPYARDS

DISUSED
AIRFIELD

STORAGE FOR
FINISHED CARS

*Marks*

KU | ES

**Reference Diagram Q6B: Location of Nissan Car Factory**

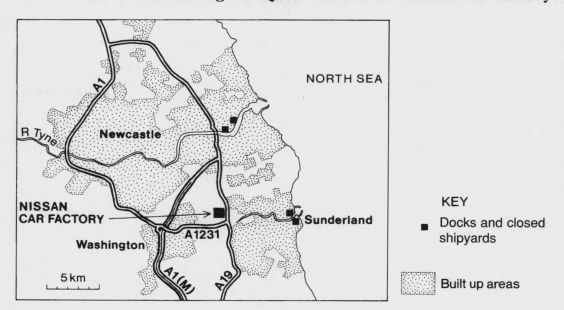

NORTH SEA

R Tyne

Newcastle

NISSAN
CAR FACTORY

Washington

A1231

Sunderland

A1(M)

A19

5 km

KEY

■ Docks and closed
shipyards

Built up areas

Study Reference Diagrams Q6A and Q6B.

Suggest reasons why Nissan chose to locate their car manufacturing plant at this site in Washington, NE England.

**7.**     **Reference Diagram Q7:  The Millennium Link Canal Project**

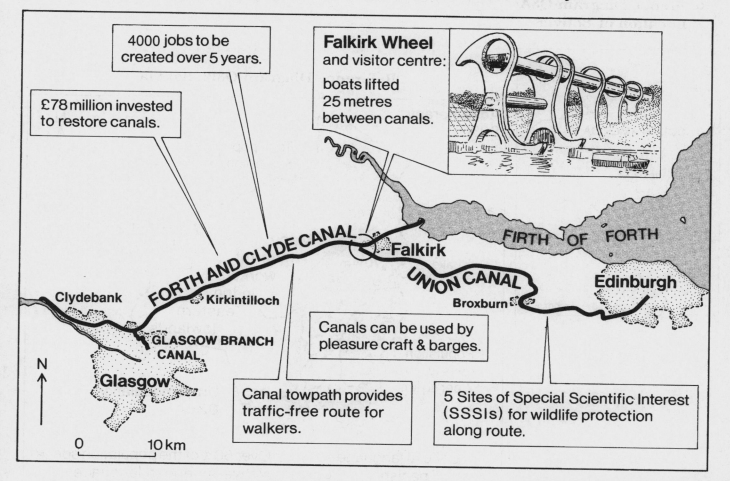

*Marks*

KU | ES

(a) Look at Reference Diagram Q7.

The Millennium Link has restored the Forth and Clyde Canal and the Union Canal in Central Scotland.  It links the estuaries of the Rivers Forth and Clyde together as well as the cities of Edinburgh and Glasgow.

Describe the benefits which the opening of the Millennium Link will have for the economy and environment of the areas around it.

5

(b) A group of geography students is researching the effects of the opening of the Millennium Link on the communities along its route.

Describe **two** gathering techniques they could use to do this.

Give reasons for your choices.

5

**[Turn over**

**8.**

**Reference Diagram Q8A:**
**Location of Bolivia**

**Reference Diagram Q8B: Bolivia**

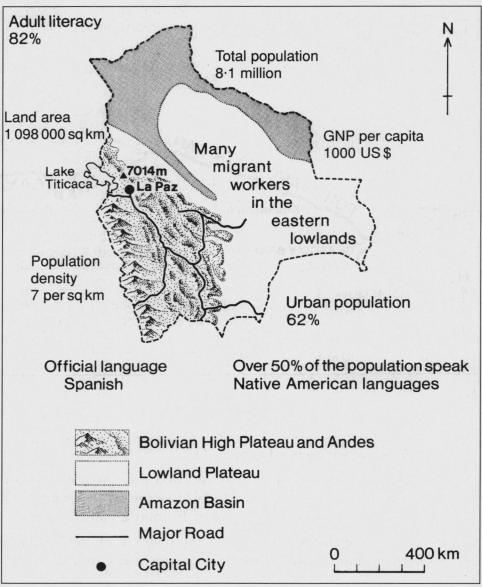

Adult literacy 82%

Total population 8·1 million

Land area 1 098 000 sq km

GNP per capita 1000 US $

Lake Titicaca ▲7014m ● La Paz

Many migrant workers in the eastern lowlands

Population density 7 per sq km

Urban population 62%

Official language Spanish

Over 50% of the population speak Native American languages

Bolivian High Plateau and Andes

Lowland Plateau

Amazon Basin

——— Major Road

● Capital City

0    400 km

*Marks*

KU   ES

Look at Reference Diagrams Q8A and Q8B.

(a) Give reasons why it may be difficult to take an accurate census in **a developing** country such as Bolivia.    5

(b) What use could the Government of **a developing** country make of population census data?    4

9.     **Reference Table Q9:  Key Mineral Exports of South Africa**

| Mineral | Percentage of World Reserves | World Rank | Percentage of World Production | World Rank |
|---------|------------------------------|------------|-------------------------------|------------|
| Chrome | 68% | 1 | 44% | 1 |
| Vermiculite | 40% | 2 | 46% | 1 |
| Gold | 39% | 1 | 21% | 1 |
| Titanium | 31% | 1 | 27% | 2 |
| Manganese | 81% | 1 | 14% | 3 |
| Uranium | 7% | 5 | 4% | 9 |

Look at Reference Table Q9.

Identify other **techniques** that could be used to **process** the data shown above.

Give reasons for your choices.

5

*[END OF QUESTION PAPER]*

# Pocket answer section for
# SQA Standard Grade Geography
# General and Credit Levels 1999 to 2003

© 2003 Scottish Qualifications Authority, All Rights Reserved
*Published by* Leckie & Leckie Ltd, 8 Whitehill Terrace, St Andrews, Scotland, KY16 8RN
tel: 01334 475656, fax: 01334 477392, enquiries@leckieandleckie.co.uk, www.leckieandleckie.co.uk

## Geography
## General Level 1999

1. *Answers worth more than 1 mark are indicated by the marks shown in brackets immediately following the statement.*

2. *A maximum 1 mark will be awarded for appropriate grid reference.*

**1.** (a)

| Feature | Letter |
|---|---|
| Woodland | B |
| North Esk River | C |
| A720 | A |
| B6482 | D |

(b) Possible answers might include:

Dalkeith House and Country Park have restricted growth to the north; Newbattle Abbey limits growth to the south; as does the golf course in square 3366; the road boundary for Dalkeith; Woodland to the north of Dalkeith restricts growth in that direction; as does the River North Esk; and to the south the River South Esk; to the east there is steep land; such as Whitehill (3566) which makes it difficult to build

(c) Possible answers might include:

It is close to a large market; both in Edinburgh and the surrounding towns such as Musselburgh, Loanhead etc; there is excellent road access; such as the A1 dual carriageway and the A720 City Bypass; there is flat land to build on; room to expand; and a labour force close by

(d) *No marks for choice*
Possible answers might include:

**Holiday Resort**:
there is a tourist information centre at 342728; there are golf courses nearby; in grid squares 3573 and 3471; tourists may visit the race course; or nearby sites of historical interest; such as the industrial museum; or the battlefield site in 3671; there is a beach

**Commuter Settlement**: it is close to Edinburgh; where there are lots of job opportunities; and commuters could drive into the city easily on roads such as the A1; or travel by rail; there does not appear to be a lot of industry in Musselburgh so many people would need to commute to get jobs (2)

**1.** (e)

| Land Use | Grid Square |
|---|---|
| Mixture of old housing and industry | 2372 |
| Central Business District (CBD) | 2573 |
| Modern housing area | 2868 |
| Older housing area | 2671 |

(f) *No marks for choice*
Answers may include:

**No** It is too close to housing estates; and the farm may suffer from vandalism; or dogs from the houses may worry the farmer's sheep; there will be a lot of noise and air pollution from the dual carriageway; the farm may lose land as the city expands outwards; and infilling takes place up to the A720

**Yes** There are excellent transport links; allowing easy access to markets; the land is gently sloping which makes it good for arable farming; it will be easy to recruit farmworkers; the farmer may make a lot of money by selling land to developers

(g) Answers may include:

**Advantages**: Dust and noise pollution will be reduced; and there may be fewer coal lorries driving through surrounding villages; making the roads safer; land can be used for useful purpose; housing, farming

**Disadvantages**: There will be less money in the local economy; and the workers may have to move away to get new jobs; or may be unemployed long term; local shops and services will suffer; the mine will become derelict; creating an eyesore for the surrounding area; freight lines will become disused

**2.** Reference must be made to a minimum of **three** weather elements.

Temperature: cold/or mild/cool/rising
Precipitation: wet/lengthy period of rain/ but **not** dry
Cloud Cover: cloudy
Wind Speed: strong wind
Wind Direction: SW/W
Reference to warm sector/font/depression/Air pressure low

# Geography
## General Level 1999 (cont.)

3. (a) **Yes** because flat floodplain; ox bow lake normally associated with lower course; river is meandering; valley slopes are gentle; there are terraces at edge of floodplain; valley floor has a very gentle gradient

       **No** because river is not very wide; floodplain is not very wide either; meanders would have bigger loops (more exaggerated) in lower course; surrounding land is too hilly for lower course

    (b) They could measure depth every 50 cm across the section line; to see if the channel is deeper on the outside bend
They could use a float to measure speed of inside and outside bend; to see if water flows faster on outside bend
They could take sketch; photo at point A; to show contrast between river cliffs and slip off slope

4. (a) Constant hot temperatures; very small range; of about 3 °C; heavy rain for most of year; humid

    (b) Logging of hardwood destroys natural habitat for many species; natural regeneration of soil halted; so less fertile. Rivers could be polluted by oil leaks; while iron ore mining causes large scale removal of soil and vegetation. Urban expansion causes more forest to be cut down.

5. *No mark for choice.*
Possible answers might include:

     **Yes** Mixture of high and low ground; north east slopes won't get much sun so not suitable for crops (2); some land far from farm buildings; so better for animals

     **No** Slopes not too steep; so crops could be grown over whole area of farm; fields are large enough for farm machinery; therefore growing crops is a possibility; town not too far away

6. Answers may include:

There are many large towns and cities nearby; which give a big market; and from which a workforce can be recruited. There are excellent communications by motorway; such as the M1 to London or the M6 to Scotland; allowing goods to be transported easily by lorry; this makes places such as Wakefield ideal locations for distribution centres; there is also good access for imports and exports by ship at Merseyside or Humberside; and by air at Manchester Airport.

7. Answers may include:

**Advantages**: People from Skye will be able to reach the mainland more easily; it may save time for emergency vehicles such as ambulances; it may encourage more tourists to visit Skye; and so boost Skye's economy; people will be able to cross even in bad weather.

**Disadvantages**: The expense will put off a lot of tourists; and so Skye will lose out; many people used to enjoy the romance of a boat trip to Skye; the cost of the tolls will prevent people on Skye from visiting the mainland as often as they would like to; some people on Skye enjoyed living on an island and didn't want to be connected to the rest of Scotland in the first place!

8. (a) Japan trades mostly with North America and Europe; exports are greater than imports; there is a trade surplus; the exports are mainly manufactured goods; the imports are mainly raw materials.

    (b) **Pie graph**—shows proportions/percentages effectively; can use shading/colour for different elements of the graph.

       **Bar graph**—gives good visual comparison between percentages; bars can be coloured differently for effect. Pie chart harder to draw due to data needing processing.

       **Divided bar graph**—shows percentages effectively; colour enhances the effect Comparative statements vis-a-vis pie charts acceptable.

9. (a) Answers may include:

the problem seems to be most serious in India/Pakistan; and in parts of the Middle East/Arabia/Yemen; Africa has a lot of underweight children; most of tropical Africa has more than 20% of its children underweight; there is a problem in Central America; and in the north and west of South America

    (b) Answers may include:

Areas where there are food shortages; because of droughts; such as parts of Africa.

In certain parts of the world mothers do not have a proper diet; so they cannot supply their babies with enough milk. In poor countries many children suffer from diseases which keep their weight down.

10. Answers may include:

the lowland area along the west coast is densely populated; the lowland area along the west coast where the land is lower than 90 metres above sea level is densely populated (2); the marshland area has a low population density; the mountain and hill areas are lightly populated; as is most of the forested area of the peninsula; river valleys such as that of Perak have dense populations.

# Geography
# General Level 2000

1. (a) *1 mark for each relevant point. 2 marks for a developed point.*

### Advantages

Beside sea loch/river; where pier has been built

Fairly flat land near shore for the CBD

Meeting of valley has made it a focus of routes

Flat land for building at Claggan

The site is in an area of fine scenery which is good for tourism

### Disadvantages

Much of Fort William is on steep slope giving building problems

Steep streets can be difficult for old people

Only a narrow strip of flat land between steep hillside and the sea

Houses will be exposed to wind

Low flat areas at Inverlochy/Nevis Bridge could suffer flooding

(b) *1 mark for each valid point. 2 marks for a developed point. Maximum 1 mark for grid references. Maximum 2 marks for list of features that have been built eg car park, gondola, chairlift, ski tow, new buildings. Maximum 3 marks if no reference to specific features on the map.*

More jobs in tourism

New structures spoil the scenery

Increased trade in the shops and hotels of Fort William

Jobs provided for the people who live in Fort William, Corpach, Caol etc

Increased traffic on A82(T)

Erosion of hillside

Disturbance to wildlife

(c)
1  Carn Beag Dearg
2  Allt a Mhuilinn
3  Carn Dearg

(d)
Arête                    1771
Hanging Valley           1869
"U" Shaped Valley        1272

(e) *1 mark for each point which explains the formation of the selected feature. A suitably annotated diagram could be awarded full marks. No marks for descriptive points.*

eg Arête

Corries eroded by ice. Corrie wall cut back towards the neighbouring corrie until a narrow ridge remains.

eg Hanging Valley

Main valley deeply eroded by glacier. Less powerful glacier in tributary valley does not erode so deeply. When ice melts a steep drop is exposed between the tributary valley and the main valley.

1. (e) continued

eg "U" Shaped Valley

Glacier/ice moves down river valley. It erodes the valley deepening it. It also straightens the valley and steepens the sides.

(f) *1 mark for each point. 2 marks for a developed point. Maximum 2 marks for list of site/location features eg flat land, timber, workforce.*

Flat land for lay-out of mill

Pier for boats taking in raw materials **or** exporting paper

Sizeable settlements provide a workforce

Railway line and main road provide transport

Local timber can provide pulp for the mill

Fresh water supply available from the Allt Dogha for cooling/processing

GR will be credited if different from original and valid

(g) *1 mark for each gathering technique. 2 marks available for explaining suitability.*

### Techniques

Take photographs of the path. Measure the width of the path at various points. Interview walkers on the West Highland Way. Study air photographs of the area. Count walkers.

### Suitability

Photos will show the bare/damaged ground. Measuring width will enable comparisons to be made at different points along the path. Walkers will be able to give an opinion about the visual damage/drainage problems along the path. By looking at air photos taken a few years apart the landscape impact would be seen. The number of walkers will give an indication of the pressure on the path.

2. *1 mark for each valid point. 2 marks for a developed point. Answers must **compare** maps/weather conditions—otherwise maximum 3 marks.*

*More than 1 weather element needed for full marks.*

Possible answers might include:

Wind speed less on Friday. 10/15 kph rising to 40/45 kph Wind direction changes from NE on Friday to S on Saturday

Temperatures lower on Friday 9/10 °C compared to 12/13 °C. Weather conditions better/clearer on Saturday

Lighter clouds on Saturday

3. *1 mark for each valid point. 2 marks for a developed point.*

Possible answers might include:

### Yes

People in new housing development will be annoyed by noise and dust from the quarry. People from caravan site may disturb wildlife in the nature reserve. View from caravan site will be spoiled by conifer plantation. Pesticides sprayed on the farmland could affect the nature reserve.

# Geography
## General Level 2000 (cont.)

**3. continued**

**No**

Nature reserve is fenced off from the caravan site and housing so it is unlikely that wildlife will be disturbed.

The farm and the nature reserve are separated by a river so farm activities will not interfere with conservation. The quarry may provide some jobs for the people in the houses. The land planted in conifers is steeply sloping so of little use to the farmer and anyway he would have to cross the river and road to get to it.

**4.** (a)    *For full marks answer must refer to both temperature and precipitation.*

Hot and mainly dry summers and warm, wet winters.

Maximum temperature 29 °C in August while minimum temperature of 9 °C in January. Temperature range is 20 °C. Highest monthly rainfall is 90 mm in December. There is drought in summer. Mediterranean climate.

(b)    *Answers must refer to both advantages and disadvantages for full marks. 1 mark for each valid point. 2 marks for a developed point.*

**Advantages**

Climate is good for tourism all year round as it is rarely too cold in winter. There will be a long growing season. Heating costs will be low.

**Disadvantages**

There will be drought in summer which will cause problems for farmers. Water shortages may occur in towns. It may be too hot to work in the middle of the day. Highest temperatures occur when there is very little rain.

**5.** (a)    *1 mark for each valid point. 2 marks for a developed point.*

Linear pattern along the lines of railways. Similar to the sector model. Growth lines radiate in all directions. Recent growth has swallowed up smaller towns like Bury so that it is now a conurbation.

(b)    *1 mark for each valid point. 2 marks for a developed point.*

Designate rural areas as Green Belt with strict planning controls on residential developments, industrial developments and new roads. Rural areas to be conserved for farming, nature reserves or SSSIs. Develop brownfield sites and build high-rise houses so that there is less need to expand. Reference to New Towns.

**6.** (a)    *1 mark for each relevant point. 2 marks for developed point.*

**No chemicals**

Higher prices available for crops produced by organic methods which do not use artificial fertilizers. Healthy eating people want organically produced products.

**Farm cottages**

No longer needed for farm workers because of the use of machinery on farms. Sale will provide income for the farmer.

**Golf Course**

Farmers are now having difficulty making a profit especially in upland areas so it is more economical to sell the land. There is an increasing demand for golf courses since more people have more leisure time.

**Cropland set-aside**

Overproduction of cereals on farms so EU pays farmers not to grow crops in some fields. Set-aside may pay better than crops in this field.

(b)    *Explanatory diagrams will be credited.*

**Technique**

Transect diagram with land-use shown on/above/below a cross section.

**Justification**

Shows any relationship between land-use and the height, slope and aspect.

**Technique**

Place an overlay with detailed land-use information over a map strip showing contours/heights.

**Justification**

Will show the relationship between height and land-use.

**7.**    *1 mark for a valid point. 2 marks for a developed point.*

**Yes**

Opportunities for an improved quality of life to be found in the city eg reliable services, ability to earn more money therefore standard of living will be better. Housing/services will be more readily available than in the country and will be a higher standard.

**No**

What people expect and what they get can be very different. Often situation is worse—no home so have to sleep in the streets/shanties. Many turn to crime to obtain money for food. May be difficult to find a job so migrant may turn to the informal sectors of employment. Often families are forced to split up. If employment is found the pay may be low as the migrants are a source of cheap labour.

**8.** (a)    *6 bars correctly drawn—        3 marks*

       *4 or 5        2 marks*

       *2 or 3        1 mark*

**8. (a) continued**

Nigeria

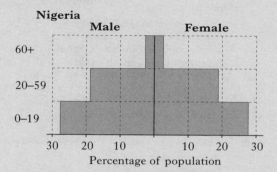

(b) *1 mark for a valid point.*
*2 marks for a developed point. Full marks cannot be obtained if only 1 country is discussed.*

Nigeria is a developing country whereas France is a Developed Country with a clean water supply, good health service, and medicine/drugs to treat illness. France also has preventative medicine in the form of vaccines. Has better living standards, smaller family size. No natural disasters such as drought which could lead to famine.

**9.** *1 mark for a valid point. 2 marks for a developed point.*

**Yes**

Most of the problems require immediate attention.

Emergency aid needed to find missing people.

Medical attention for diseases would be a priority.

Need to rescue people in the capital city who were cut off.

Long term aid will not rescue people from the mudslides.

Most crops lost, so urgent food supplies will be necessary—can't wait for a new harvest.

**No**

Central America will take years to recover, so long term aid is essential.

Replacement crops will take time to regrow.

Most of the roads and buildings are ruined but these may take months to rebuild.

Tree cutting is a major cause of soil erosion, but reafforestation to protect soils is a long term project.

Both types of aid are necessary.

**10.** *Maximum 1 mark for a "direct lift". 1 mark for each valid point. 2 marks for a developed point.*

If there is only one currency, saves problem/expense of changing money when you go abroad.

Easier to compare prices without having to convert currencies.

Fewer delays at borders makes travel more convenient and quicker. This could cut costs for companies that have a lot of business in Europe. People will be free to look for jobs in other European countries, since only non EU citizens need permits.

# Geography
# General Level 2001

**1.** (a) *1 mark for a valid point.*
*2 marks for a developed point. Answers must relate to differences. This could be in two separate paragraphs.*

Dennistoun has a grid iron street pattern, but Castlemilk has crescents.

Dennistoun is close to the city centre, but Castlemilk is on the outskirts.

Dennistoun has less open space than Castlemilk. Dennistoun probably has nineteenth century housing or tenements whereas Castlemilk could have houses with gardens or blocks of multi-story flats.

(b) *1 mark for a valid point.*
*2 marks for a developed point. Maximum of 1 mark for appropriate use of grid references.*

The shopping centre lies on the motorway junction near to M8 so good access; there is plenty of land to build on; note the importance of car parking; in a large built up area so lots of customers will come; not in the city centre so easier to get to; flat land to build on.

(c) *1 mark for a valid point. 2 marks for a developed point. Maximum of 1 mark for appropriate use of grid references.*

Warehouses;

Railway sidings;

Large factory blocks;

Docks;

Works.

(d) *1 mark for a valid point. 2 marks for a developed point. Maximum of 1 mark for appropriate use of grid references.*

**Advantages**—extension will make it quicker for people in places like Thornliebank to get to city centre for work/shopping; fewer cars will need to go through housing areas, so it will be safer for local residents; less congestion.

**Disadvantages**—extension goes through part of Pollock Country Park (GR 5558); spoils amenity; trees need to be cut down; road seems to split up areas of housing eg Corkerhill.

(e) *1 mark for a valid point. 2 marks for a developed point. Maximum of 1 mark for appropriate use of grid references.*

The Clyde is a barrier to communications eg all the traffic has to flow across a few bridges. The Clyde may flood eg in 5267.

The Clyde provides opportunities eg flat flood plain suited to building on; river can be used by ships for trade; people may want to live in a waterfront location.

# Geography
## General Level 2001 (cont.)

**2.** *1 mark per valid explanation.*
*2 marks for a developed point. Full marks could be obtained from well annotated diagram(s).*

Possible answers may include:

Ox-bow lakes are formed in the lower course of the river where meandering happens. There is erosion on the outside of the bend and sediment builds up on the inside of the bend, cutting off the Lake.

**3.** (*a*)    *4 correct—3 marks*
*2 or 3 correct—2 marks*
*1 correct—1 mark*

1 = Tundra
2 = Equatorial Rainforest
3 = Hot Desert
4 = Mediterranean

(*b*)    (i)    *1 mark for choice*
Climate = Tundra

(ii)    *1 mark for a valid point.*
*2 marks for a developed point.*

Low rainfall; Large temperature range; negative temperatures; summer temperatures below 10° C

**4.** *1 mark per valid point. 2 marks for a developed point.*

**Yes**
There is an oil shortage and this area has lots of fossil fuels. No humans will be affected by the mining operations because nobody lives here. Increasing world population means that resources such as these will have to be developed.

**No**
Antarctica is unspoiled and developing its resources will damage the environment. There is a lot of marine life such as whales and these would be harmed by pollution—oil leaks etc. Antarctica should be left as a natural wilderness. The sea is often frozen and this would make drilling for oil difficult. Ships would not get in during winter to transport materials. Harsh weather would make working in Antarctica very unpleasant.

**5.** (*a*)    *1 mark for each valid point.*
*2 marks for a developed point.*

**Advantages**
Higher yields so more food. Large field size means big machines can be used efficiently. Big farm units mean farmers can produce enough to earn a good living. Firms have set up to supply and maintain modern farm machines and this provides employment in rural areas.

Labour costs are now a smaller proportion of farm inputs.

**5. (*a*) continued**

**Disadvantages**
Enlargement of fields has meant the removal of field boundaries such as hedges and wildlife has suffered. Increased use of machines has resulted in the loss of farm workers' jobs. Farm chemicals have improved crop yields but can be bad for wildlife and sometimes pollute streams and rivers.

(*b*)    *1 mark per technique. 2 marks available for justification.*

**Techniques** eg
Pie chart/bar chart;
colour coded land use map;
overlays;
scattergraph;
annotated cross-section

**Justifications** eg
Pie chart/divided bar chart can be used to show the proportion of the farm devoted to each land use. Colouring the map will show the land use pattern on the farm. An overlay can be used to show the link between slope and land use. Scattergraph shows nature of relationship between field size and slope (degrees). Annotated cross-section gives a clear indication of land use and changes in relief on the same diagram.

**6.** (*a*)    *1 mark per valid point. 2 marks for a developed point.*

Walkers will create more footpath erosion. Tourists create problems for farmers by leaving gates open and can harm wildlife by dropping litter. Too many people will spoil the peace and quiet. Rare Alpine plants may be trampled and walkers may get into difficulties in bad weather and need rescuing.

(*b*)    *1 mark for a valid point.*
*2 marks for a developed point. Must have techniques and justifications for full marks.*

**Techniques** eg
Taking photos at different heights; take information from an OS map; transect study; interview farmers/other land users; fieldsketches.

**Justifications** eg
Photos/OS map/transect studies—allows comparison, shows content; the farmer will know why they use the land in different ways.

**7.** *1 mark for each valid point. 2 marks for a developed point.*

Government efforts made to attract new industry/creating employment eg government/EU grants to encourage new developments; cheap loans; retraining programmes for workers; Scottish Enterprise to prepare incentive packages; environmental schemes to improve the image of old industrial areas and make them attractive to modern high-tech industry.

**8.**   *(a)*   *1 mark for a valid point.*
*2 marks for a developed point.*

Award a maximum of two marks for simplistic statements about totals eg in developed countries, total population will go from 1·18 billion to 1·16 billion people.

Give credit for developed points eg in developed countries, total population will fall slightly between 1998 and 2050, from 1·18 billion to 1·16 billion people.

*(b)*   *1 mark for a valid point.*
*2 marks for a developed point.*

More people will make it harder to get a job, so many families will not be able to afford to buy food and clothes; the government will have to provide more schools, so taxes will have to go up; lack of housing, more shanty towns; food production unable to meet demand.

**9.**   *(a)*   *1 mark for each of two correctly placed lines to create three segments.*
*1 mark for correctly labelling all four segments.*

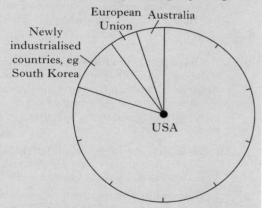

*(b)*   *1 mark for each valid point. Maximum of 2 marks for straight lift.*

It produces a high number of important exports which many other countries need; it has the seventh largest population in the world so will have a large workforce to draw on.

**10.**   *No marks for choice. 1 mark for each valid point in favour of choice, or against the other two rejected options. 2 marks for a developed point.*

Option A—many babies are ill, so emergency medicines might help them; you need to help people before you start teaching them or building dams; they have no crops so they have no choice but to get emergency aid.

Option B—many of their problems could be helped with education; most people cannot read or write, so they won't learn how to grow better crops; very few children have the chance to go to school, so they cannot get on in life; emergency aid just makes them too dependent—they want to be self-reliant; dam would take too long, and be wasteful.

Option C—emergency aid just makes them too dependent—they want to be self-reliant; helps crops grow; maybe stop mothers having to walk miles for water.

# Geography
# General Level 2002

*1. Answers worth more than 1 mark are indicated by the marks shown in brackets immediately following the statement.*

*2. A maximum 1 mark will be awarded for appropriate grid reference.*

**1.**   *(a)*

| Descriptions | Cross-section Letter |
|---|---|
| Outskirts of town | C |
| Woodland | D |
| Villages/farmland | A |
| Pasture | B |

*(b)*   **River**: Meanders; particularly between bridges at Ross-on-Wye. Flowing southwards. Approaching 100 metres wide. Gentle river gradient.

**Valley**: Wide floodplain. Drainage ditches on floor of floodplain. Valley sides fairly gentle but steeper at certain places such as west bank in 5826. Floodplain can reach over 500 metres in width in square 5826 (2). Small tributary stream joins Wye near Benhall. Valley appears a shallow U-shape.

*(c)*   *Techniques*: eg Measure width, depth and speed of river. Measure width of river and measure speed by timing floats passing through a measured distance. Using an Ordnance Survey map. Take photographs; draw field sketches. Interview people who live beside the river.

*Justification*: eg Measurements can be compared with others taken at a different time or at other places on the course of the river. People interviewed can provide eye witness information about floods/course changes. Photographs taken can be compared with older photographs of the same stretch of the river. The measurements can be used to work out the area of the stream channel and the amount/volume of water carried (2).

*(d)*   *No marks for choice.*
**Livestock**: Close to Ross-on-Wye for sale of milk. Areas of marsh suggest farm better for grass than crops as wet soils may be a problem (2).

**Arable**: Most of the land is below 60 m above sea level. Most of the slopes are fairly gentle so machinery could be easily operated (2).

**Mixed**: Some quite steep land which would be better kept as grazing. Wet areas would be expensive to drain for crops. Drier and more gently sloping land would have good soil for crop growing.

*(e)*   No: Sellack only has minor road links which are unlikely to be suitable for big lorries.

# Geography
# General Level 2002 (cont.)

## 1. (e) continued

Waste from reopened quarries may pollute the river. Blasting and big lorries may threaten the historic "cross" at Sellack. Removal of areas of woodland will be bad for wildlife.

Yes: Roads can be upgraded to make them suitable for big lorries. Very few people live close to the quarries. Will provide employment in local area. Woodland will help screen quarry at 561277 (2).

(f) **Advantages**:

Slightly higher land comes closer to river making flood plain easier to cross. Old crossing point on River Wye as shown by Wilton bridge at 590243. As a result routes converged on Ross-on-Wye bringing business and resulting in growth of town (2). Site beside the River Wye is scenic and benefits modern tourist industry.

**Disadvantages**:

Part of the old town close to the river has a high flood risk as it is on flat land below the 35 metre contour (2). It is on the outside of the river bend so erosion protection is necessary.

(g) *No marks for choice.*
**Holiday Resort**: Historic town, Wilton Bridge and Wilton Castle at 590243 and 590244. Camp and caravan site. Facilities such as a Museum.

**Market Town**: Lot of farms in surrounding area. Focus of routes so easy to get to and a good place for business to develop (3).

**Industrial Town**: Industrial estate on the edge of town beside the A40 and the former railway line (3). The link to the M50 will make it an attractive location for industry. Possible location for food processing industries with many farms in the area eg Poultry farm in square 6026 and also the orchards (4).

## 2. (a)

| Feature | Letter |
|---|---|
| Drumlin | C |
| Outwash Plain | A |
| Esker | D |
| Terminal Moraine | B |

(b) **Outwash Plain**: Streams pouring from melting ice carry sands and small stones spread over a wide area laid down in layers (4).

**Esker**: Stream flowing in tunnel under ice. Sands/stones choke the tunnel when ice melts a long sandy ridge left parallel to direction of former glacier (4).

**Drumlin**: These are formed within ice; material is dumped by glacier; left as series of low hills—egg shaped

**Terminal Moraine**: Loose material is carried by glacier; this is dumped when ice melts; material is left at the end of the glacier; this shows the maximum extent of glacier.

## 3. (a)
Hot desert: Graph 2. Equatorial Rainforest: Map area D. Mediterranean: Graph 1. Tundra: Map area A

(b) Graph 3 (Tundra)
Minimum temperatures are below −25 °C. Average temperatures below freezing for 8/9 months or only 3/4 months above freezing. Average temperature of the warmest month is only 9/10 °C. Annual precipitation is very low although there is some in every month (2). Less than 400 mm of precipitation per year. The climate is that of a cold desert.

## 4.
Failure of rainfall and high evaporation rate. Overgrazing by cattle/goats/sheep. Cultivation where rainfall low. Clearing of woodland areas for firewood.

## 5.
The higher the land the lower the temperatures. Lowest temperatures in North West Highlands and Grampians. Temperatures also low in the Southern Uplands. Mild conditions along west coast where temperatures are above 6 °C on the lower land (2). Less cold conditions on lowlands around the Firth of Forth.

## 6. (a)
19th century area has a grid-iron pattern whereas the 20th century area has a curved geometric pattern (2). Housing density greater in the 19th century area than in modern area. Gardens in evidence in 20th century area.

(b) Draw field sketches; take photographs of buildings and street scenes in two areas to enable comparison of their appearance (2).

Carry out traffic surveys to compare possible pedestrian hazards (2) and air pollution in the two areas.

Make observations on such things as bad housing, noise, graffiti, litter (2) and award points for each to allow a numerical index to be calculated to enable a comparison between the two areas (2).

## 7. (a)
Flat land for building and room for expansion (2). Plenty space for parking. Good road transport such as the A19 dual carriageway allows quick and easy access for lorries (2). Nearby housing estate for workers. Ready made buildings for companies to move into. Recreation facilities for key workers.

(b) Alternative employment to replace declining traditional industries. High-tech companies improve the image of the area and may attract other firms (2). New industries nearby will provide opportunities for local young people and stop them moving away to find work (2). High wages paid by modern companies put money into the local economy.

8. (a) In developing countries large numbers have migrated from countryside to cities. Problems of poverty and lack of educational opportunity in rural areas. Cities have drawn people because they have industries providing employment. The range of services in cities also attract people from rural areas. In developing countries many feel that moving to the city will result in a better life.

(b) Pie charts could be drawn for each year and the urban population segment shaded or given a colour (2). The differences in segment size would clearly bring out the changes in the proportion of the population living in urban areas.

Four horizontal bar charts set one above the other. The percentage of the population for each year to be shown as a shaded; coloured section of the bar graph. Changes in the urban share of total population can be easily seen and compared.

9. **Advantages**: Larger market to sell goods into without being subject to tariffs (2). Access to a wider range of resources. Members of a trade alliance can protect own industry from cheaper imports by levying a tax on goods from non-member countries (2).

**Disadvantages**: Some of the rules of the alliance may not suit all member countries. Protecting industry in member countries means that the people may have to pay more for goods such as foodstuffs which would be cheaper at world prices (3). There may be disputes between members over the share-out of resources such as fish in the EU (2).

10. Intermediate projects tend to be low cost. Do not require large amounts of foreign aid in the form of money or expertise and as a result are unlikely to be affected by tied aid arrangements (3). Based on local resources and materials and this keeps cost down. Make use of abundant local labour and do not require highly trained workers. Do not rely on expensive fossil fuels.

# Geography
# General Level 2003

*Please note:*
- *Points that will gain marks are separated by semicolons (";").*
- *Developed points, appropriate examples and relevant grid references are worth 2 marks. These are noted in the following answer guide with "(2)".*
- *Your answers do not have to include all the points given in the following answer guide. However, to gain high marks, your answers must include enough points to cover the number of marks available for each question.*

1. (a) *One mark for any valid point.*
Focus of main roads (eg A721); area has buildings packed close together there is a main railway station; large number of churches and civic buildings are close by. Heritage centre. No marks for grid references.

(b) *Comparisons must be made for full marks.*
Sunnyside has a grid-iron pattern of streets while Carnbroe has more varied pattern of curving streets which will be less monotonous (2); in Sunnyside the streets are long and allow through traffic while in Carnbroe there are short streets with many in the form of a cul-de-sac (2); which is much safer; Sunnyside is in the centre of the built-up area while Carnbroe is on the outskirts (2); in Sunnyside the land is all built up while there is open space round Carnbroe. Reference to specific buildings.

Or any other valid point.

(c) *Answer must mention both for full marks.*
**Advantages**: the land is gently flat sloping, so easy to farm; it's a south facing slope which may be suitable for crops; it's beside a main road (A89) so has good transport facilities for bringing in supplies and sending produce to market (2); it's close to urban markets.

**Disadvantages**: growth of new housing areas or roads may lead to loss of land; pylons may restrict use of machinery; there may be noise or fumes from main road, may be nuisance/vandalism problems from adjacent urban areas.

Or any other valid point.

(d) (i) Area on old map almost all built-up, now very little of area built up; steel works are no longer marked (though there is a "wks"); large buildings/factories have been removed; as have railway sidings or all railways except main line; there used to be chimneys/cooling towers/storage tanks which are no longer there; More roads.

(ii) Questionnaire given to local residents to obtain information about impact on employment. Reason: questionnaires can be issued to a large number of people; and if enough are returned they should give results based on a representative sample of the population; Older residents will have knowledge of changes which have occurred.

Visit area and record appearance (in notebook, sketch or photograph). Reason: present appearance can be compared with old photographs to assess impact of change

Similarly questionnaires could be used to investigate effects on local environment.

# Geography
# General Level 2003 (cont.)

## 1. (d) (ii) continued

Interview local shop keepers/business persons to find out impact of change on the economy. Reason: such people will have records of past and present levels of custom/spending; and will be able to identify change in the form of effects on their business.

Calculate an environmental quality index by giving scores/points to features in an area. Reason: this can then be compared with scores for areas which still have heavy industry; this might indicate effects of change on the environment.

(e) attractions might include:
Visitor centre; picnic site; camping and caravanning site; water sports centre; theme park.

(f) Clyde is a winding, meandering river (eg 7455); general direction is SE to NW; number of lakes (eg 761540) which may indicate drainage difficulties; gentle gradient (doesn't cross contour lines); valley floor/flood plain very wide; up to ½ km wide (eg 7653); valley sides gentler on SW side and steeper on NE (eg in 7654); valley sides rise from about 30m to 100m; or other relevant points.

## 2. (a)
Slopes in upper course are much steeper; Valley is much narrower in upper course; River in lower course is much wider than in the upper course; Wide flood plain in lower course whereas there is no flood plain. Tributaries. V-shaped profile in upper course, whereas much broader shallower valley.

(b) **Upper course**: climbing because there are very steep slopes with rocky outcrops; sheep graze the steep slopes because they are hardy and can cope with difficult terrain.

**Lower course**: much lower and level therefore easier to grow crops; road and rail can use the flat land beside the river; rivers may deposit fertile silt; which allows crops to grow.

## 3. (a)
Painted white: this reflects sunlight.
Legs 1 m long: prevents thermometers being affected by ground temperatures.

Placed on grass: neutral surface does not cause air above it to be warmer/colder than surrounding air.

Made of wood: wood is poor conductor of heat so screen won't overheat and give exaggerated reading.

Slatted sides: allows air to circulate freely so outside air can reach thermometer; also keep out direct rays of sun; so thermometer isn't directly heated.

(b) Temperatures in south and east are higher because this area is in the warm sector of the depression; and has more sunshine, temperatures in north and west are colder because this area is in the area behind cold front; has more cloud so less sunshine; and areas further north tend to be colder on average because of their latitude/greater distance from equator.

## 4. (a)

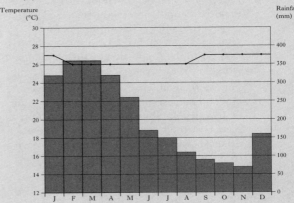

(b) constant warm temperatures; between 26 °C and 27 °C each month; rain all year; heaviest rain from January to April; T.R.F. Climate.

(c) **Environment**: soil erosion, increased risk of gulleys; contamination of soil and rivers by mining; loss of plant/animal habitat; rainfall slowly declines.

**People**: native Amerindians lose hunting territory; roads encourage increased settlement of the Rain Forest, leading to further destruction of Indian land (2).

## 5. *Negative points for rejected options are acceptable.*

A: deep water.

B: flat land; reasonably close to city.

C: deep water; close to city; only 12 km from city boundary; sheltered from wind/high seas on flat land.

D: shelter; reasonably close to city; only 12 km from boundary; flat land.

E: deep water; flat land.

## 6. (a)
Your answer should refer to push factors eg difficult life in rural areas; land too poor to farm; not enough land for everyone; lack of schools, medical care etc; no jobs apart from farming.

(b) **Yes**: able to send money back to family; improving living standards at home; jobs available; some people who move seem to manage well.

**6.** (*b*) **continued**

**No**: rents of available housing too expensive; for workers with low wages; not enough housing for number of migrants; so shanty towns grow; probably with worse living conditions than in the countryside; open sewers common.

**7.** (*a*) Money/wealth concentrated in Developed world countries; eg USA, Japan and Europe; small country of Switzerland important centre of world finance; countries such as Japan and USA have highly educated people; required to manage large companies; rest of world has mainly branches of large companies; which are established there to supply a market; or because of lower labour costs; companies want to keep their decision making headquarters in the part of the world where they started up (2).

Or any other valid points.

(*b*) **Technique**: eg bar graphs; divided graphs; pie chart; table; shading of world map.

**Reasons**: divided bar graph: each section of the bar drawn in proportion to number of headquarters in that part of the world; easy to compare relative importance of different parts of the world as location for headquarters; different colours or shading techniques will enhance visual comparison.

Pie chart presents effective visual picture to compare importance of different parts of the world; size of segments in direct proportion to importance of different parts of the world.

Bar graph easy to work out actual number of companies quickly by referring to scale of bar graph; different bar heights make virtual comparison easy; comparison enhanced by shading/colour; bar graph can be superimposed on to world map.

Or any other valid justification.

**8.** **short term**: help needed right away; mainly food, medicine, shelter; to prevent people dying; need help to find injured, buried people in rubbish.

**long term**: better if buildings made more earthquake proof; takes time and money to do; most buildings and services need to be replaced; which can't be done immediately.

Or any other valid point.

# Geography
## Credit Level 1999

*1. Answers worth more than 1 mark are indicated by the marks shown in brackets immediately following the statement.*

*2. A maximum 1 mark will be awarded for appropriate grid reference.*

**1.** (*a*) (i) A: Watendlath
B: Launchy Gill
C: Thirlmere
D: Swirral Edge

(ii) Marks will be given for relevant points made in diagram form.

**U-shaped valley:**
Reference to preglacial landscape will be credited

Created by glacial erosion. As glacier moved down valley rock fragments became frozen into the base of glacier and were plucked away as the ice moved on (2). Ground moraine scraped over the land surface abrading it (2). As a result the valley became steeper, straighter and wider.

**Hanging valley:**
These were created by movement of glacier through main valley; glacier widened and deepened main valley leaving sides high and steep; tributary valley was left high above main valley; river channel flowed down steep slope into main valley when ice retreated.

**Arête:**
Formed by corries forming back to back on sides of mountain; as corries deepened into mountain sides they were separated by a steep ridge (2). This steep ridge is called an arête.

(*b*) The main cluster of population is at Keswick which is a natural focus of routes where services have grown (2). Most settlement is associated with valleys and lake shores where there are routeways and flat land (2). Large areas of mountain and moorland with steep slopes and access problems do not support a resident population (2). Farm buildings are found on valley floors where there is flat land. Clusters of population are associated with small settlements such as Rosthwaite at minor road junctions. In the north west of the extract people live in villages at the foot of the hills but above the level of flood danger (eg Appelthwaite at GR2625) (2). No settlement/population where the lake is.

(*c*) (i) **Advantages:**

eg It is accessible because it is a route centre and there is a bus station (2). Keswick has plenty amenities such as the museum, youth hostel, information centre, caravan and campsite (2). Attractive scenery such as lakes, woodlands, rivers. Close to Derwentwater for water sports. Opportunity for hillwalking in surrounding hills and rock climbing on cliffs of Borrowdale (2). Sited on low land so is more sheltered and not as wet as the surrounding mountains.

# Geography
# Credit Level 1999 (cont.)

## 1. (c) (i) continued

**Disadvantages:**

There is no railway link, reducing accessibility and possibly increasing congestion on roads to Keswick (2). Keswick is in a mountainous area so the weather is often cool and wet due to relief rainfall (2). There is no evidence of antiquities in the immediate vicinity of Keswick.

(ii) Compile a questionnaire and use it to interview shopkeepers in Keswick asking them how much of their business depends on tourists (2). The questionnaire would mean up to date data would be gathered which is unlikely to be available from published sources (2).

Carry out a series of traffic surveys at various times of the year on roads such as the B5289 (2). The data collected will enable judgements to be made about roads and locations suffering pressures from increased traffic during the tourist season (2).

Observe tourist related land uses in the area around Keswick and record them by taking a series of photographs.

Photographs will provide a basis for assessing in laboratory or classroom conditions the environmental impact of selected tourist developments. Scenes can also be compared with older photographic or map evidence.

Or any other valid examples with justification.

## 2.
Small streams in upland areas receive a supply of rainwater or water from further upstream (2). This water has energy which it uses to carry/move large loads and this results in the river cutting (eroding) down (vertically) (2). Stones going round and round can form pot holes in the stream bed. The valley slope is gradually worn away by the weather and loose soil and rocks fall down the steep slope or are washed down by rainfall (2). The river carries this material downstream. Rocks on the valley side can be broken down by frost or by chemical weathering (2).

## 3.
(a) Many rivers discharge into the Mediterranean and they carry effluent and farm waste (2). There is very heavy oil tanker traffic causing pollution. Oil refineries on the Mediterranean coast mean spillages are likely. The Mediterranean is almost enclosed by land so tides/currents are unlikely to be strong enough to break up oil slicks and other pollutants (2). There is high population density along much of the Mediterranean so domestic waste/sewage disposal is a problem

## 3. (a) continued

Great numbers of tourists visit the coastline producing a lot of waste.

(b) **For:**
Many countries share the coast of the Mediterranean so they have common interest/responsibility. Many problems start in one country and are then carried to other countries by rivers and sea currents. An example is fertiliser washed down the river Po polluting the coastline of the Adriatic Sea. Tourists would benefit from cleaner beaches.

**Against:**
Some countries are not on friendly terms and are unlikely to agree to the proposal. Some countries may not be able to afford the anti-pollution measures. Tankers from countries from outside the Mediterranean use the Mediterranean sea routes and cause pollution. Many countries rely on oil and may be worried about measures likely to make it more expensive.

## 4.
Line graphs (temperature) drawn for Glasgow and Stornoway will show *the temperature trends for the week and enable the daily differences between Glasgow and Stornoway to be clearly seen/ calculated* (3).

Bar graph/histogram (rainfall) *will show the daily amount of rain. Statistics for both places can be shown on the same graph using different shading allowing comparisons to be made* (3).

Pie charts (sunshine) could be drawn for each day to show *the percentage of each day with sunshine. Sunshine segments can be coloured to make the comparison clearer* (3).

Wind rose (wind) *conveys effective visual impression of direction combined with frequency* (2).

## 5.
Farming: Farmer could use some of the hills for grazing sheep, as they are hardy and can cope with rough weather, they can find enough grazing there and the land is too steep for machinery. (2) Some of the land could be used for commercial forestry as the soils are not good enough for crops. The fields closest to the farm might be used for sheep in winter when there is too much snow on the hills and where, during the worst snow, the farmer can get extra food easily to them (2).

Non farming: To earn extra income the farmer could sell permits for fishing in the loch and charge for allowing people to shoot grouse on his moorland (2). The disused cottages formerly used for farmworkers could be rented out. The farmer could charge tourists for camping in one of his fields and run bed and breakfast in the farmhouse (2).

6. Government assistance is available at this site which could save the Company millions of pounds. Close to several motorways which will allow easy access and enable quick transport of goods to and from the factory (2). Edinburgh Airport will allow executives to travel quickly to meetings elsewhere. The site is close to towns such as Dunfermline which will supply a workforce. Many workers made redundant by the closure of Rosyth will be looking for work. The site is close enough to colleges and universities to allow the company to cooperate with them on research projects.

7. *No marks for choice.*
   **Yes**:
   China's share of world trade is growing much faster. It has a huge population, providing a massive labour force, and potential market (3). It has much lower labour costs which will encourage investment (2).

   **No**:
   Its trade figures are much lower at the moment. Literacy in China is much lower so it is unlikely that a less well educated workforce will produce more than literate countries like Japan and the USA (2). It is not as big as the USA, so it is unlikely to have more natural resources than it can exploit (2).

8. (a) Poverty and food shortages push people out of rural areas, to seek what they think will be a better life in the city. There is more scope to earn money in the city in informal jobs such as water selling or car "attendance" (2). Young people are attracted by the exciting image of a big city. Schooling and medical facilities are more likely to be available in the city (2). Housing may be bad but improvements are taking place in many shanty towns. Piped water and sanitation are more likely to be available in the city than in most rural settlements (2).

   (b) Large numbers of people have moved out of inner city areas of large cities because of the run-down environment of these areas (2). Better off people can afford to commute to the city and prefer to live in smaller settlements where there is less congestion and noise (2). New towns have been built outside many large cities and they provide modern housing and work (2). Crime and vandalism has driven a lot of people out of the large cities.

9. Approach A: HEP can be used in new industries, providing jobs (2). A very large area of land can be irrigated, so many people will benefit as more crops can be grown (3).
   Approach B: This is much cheaper, and uses the skills of local people. Large numbers of people will not have to be resettled. Vast areas of farmland will not be lost. Less likelihood of soils becoming saline.

10. *No marks for choice.*
    **Yes**: If Developing country becomes more affluent it will import more goods from the Developed country thus improving employment prospects in the Developed country because production will increase (3). Aid can be tied so that Developing country must buy goods from the Developed country (3). Five Developed countries have exceeded the UN target figure and a small percentage of a developed country's GNP is a lot of money (2).

    **No**: Developed country cannot compete with the cheap products of the Developing country leading to unemployment in the Developed country (2) or the Developed country is forced to put import taxes on products coming from the Developing country so that less of these goods will sell and the income of the Developing country will fall (3). The Developing country can no longer afford to buy products from the Developed country and industry in the Developed country will suffer (2). Only a small percentage of the GNP of Developed countries is spent on Aid and very few countries have reached the UN target figure (2).

# Geography Credit
# Level 2000

1. (a) *1 mark for choice of grid square.*
       *1 mark for each piece of supporting evidence.*
       *No extra mark for 6 figure grid reference. If wrong square chosen, may pick up marks for relevant reasons.*

       Grid square 4920 contains most of CBD.

       Answers might include:

       There is a ring road around three sides of CBD in this square; it has a main Railway Station at 496207; there is a Town Hall and Tourist Information Centre, several churches and a bus station.

   (b) *1 mark per valid point. 2 marks per expanded point. Detailed information about techniques and justification **must** be given.*

       **Techniques**
       Possible answers might include:

       Carry out survey using land use maps; go to planning office to find out about industrial change in the area; consult in libraries for information; interview residents/industry owners in the area; use photos to show comparisons in landscape then and now.

       **Justifications**
       Survey will be up to date and more accurate; planning office have very recent accurate data; libraries will have several sources of information.

# Geography Credit
# Level 2000 (cont.)

1.  (c)  *1 mark for each relevant statement. 2 marks for a developed point.*

Answers might include:

Linthorpe is an inner city area while Nunthorpe is on the outskirts; Linthorpe and Marton Grove will have older housing; and possibly quite a bit of old industry; it has an old street pattern (grid iron) at 488188; while Nunthorpe's is much newer; with many cul de sacs indicating modern housing areas; Linthorpe is likely to be more crowded area; while Nunthorpe will have bigger gardens and more open green areas.

(d)  *1 mark for each relevant statement. 2 marks for a developed point.*

*Maximum 1 mark for grid references.*

Answers **must** refer to map evidence for full marks and might include:

Teesport is well situated for trade with the rest of Europe across the North Sea; and is also conveniently located to take advantage of North Sea oil and gas; which will be an important raw material in industries such as petrochemicals. There is a huge area of flat land around the Tees estuary which is good for building factories on; these will benefit from nearby labour force in towns such as Middlesborough and Billingham; and the good harbour facilities along the Tees for imports/exports by sea. There are sheltered docks for ships (545235) and deep for the largest vessels; there are excellent facilities for transporting goods to and from factories by road such as A66 dual carriagway and also by rail as shown by the many freight railways eg 5623.

(e)  *Valley **and** river course must both be mentioned for full marks, otherwise maximum 3 marks. 1 mark per valid point. 2 marks per expanded point.*

Possible answers might include:

Wide meanders; right hand bend at 4419; wide river in its lower course; embankments at 4416 to prevent flooding; abandoned meanders at ox bow lake at 464193; tidal after barrage

Wide floodplain; particularly further downstream.

(f)  *1 mark for each relevant statement. 2 marks for a developed point.*

1. (f) continued

**Advantages**—there is already a large area of marsh with wildlife, which is worth protecting; visitors will be able to get to site easily on existing A class roads; there are already developments such as Cowpen Bewley Country Park close by; so an International Nature Reserve would fit in well; and ensure that the oil terminals and chemical works to the east do not expand over this area; freshwater lakes and saltwater mud flats.

**Disadvantages**—this site is very close to big heavy industries; which might cause serious damage to the Nature Reserve; from either air pollution or leaks of oil and chemicals into the waterways and marshes; it might take up land which could be used for industrial development; resulting in lost job opportunities for the area; there are far too many power cables across this site which would not look good in a Nature Reserve;  Flooding from sea.

2.  *1 mark per valid point. 2 marks per expanded point. Fronts and east and west **must** be referred to in their answer. Maximum 2 marks for description.*

Possible answers might include:

Cold front down length of western Britain N–S linked to band of rain cloud; and low temperature; east coast in warm sector so; temperatures on east generally higher, conditions drier, outbreaks of sunshine; particularly in SE England; warm front moving into Ireland so cloud and rain developing; stronger winds in west shown by closer isobars.

3.  (a)  *1 mark for each relevant statement. 2 marks for a developed point.*

**Yes:** the mountain railway will allow more skiers to get on to the ski slopes which will help the economy of Aviemore and the local area as more money is spent at the Cairngorm Ski Centre and in local shops and businesses; the railway itself will become a tourist attraction with the same effect; existing ski tows and chairlifts will be removed so that visual impact of the railway projects will be reduced; ski related jobs will be safeguarded and new jobs may be created; there will be a boom period for local construction workers.

**No:** construction of the railway may damage the environment; the visual impact will detract from the splendour of the Cairngorms; increased numbers of visitors on the Cairngorm Plateau will pose a threat to the National Nature Reserve; trampling may cause erosion or damage rare plants; there may be more accidents on the ski slopes with an increased number of skiers; there may be more hillwalking accidents as more people gain access to the mountains by rail.

3.   (b)   Possible answers could include:

The students could interview local residents in the Aviemore area to find out whether they had noticed a change in the number of tourists; this would allow comparisons to be made; about the number of tourists and also the seasonal distribution of tourists. They could do a study of occupancy rates; to find out about any increase in tourist numbers; they could also compare photographs of Cairngorm before and after the railway was built; to assess the visual impact. They could try to access information from agencies such as SNH to find out whether wildlife in the National Nature Reserve, such as ptarmigan, had been affected. Measurements of footpath width could be made and compared with previous data to assess possible footpath erosion.

Answers may include reference to physical environmental, economic or human impact.

4.   *1 mark per valid point. 2 marks for a developed point.*

Possible answers could include:

**Advantages**—more jobs/lower unemployment; more jobs in science based industries mean fewer Irish graduates have to emigrate; higher living standards; increased prosperity brings more money into shops and hotels; tourists will sustain many remote communities; eg in the far west.

**Disadvantages**—too much dependence on foreign firms is dangerous; as they may decide to pull out; and this will result in unemployment; most of the benefits may be restricted to a few areas of the country; tourism may threaten the environment; and also the culture of certain areas; cost of subsidising foreign investment; effect on local firms.

5.   *No marks for choice. 1 mark for each relevant statement. 2 marks for developed point.*

Possible answers might include:

**Yes:** Oil has brought lots of benefits to Nigeria which outweigh disadvantages—these include jobs for 25,000 people; allowing Nigerians to improve their standards of living; oil accounts for 90% of Nigeria's exports; indicating that without it Nigeria's balance of trade would be much poorer; there have been benefits for local people as oil companies have invested money in local projects; although there has been some environmental damage, the health, education and wealth of local people have benefited enormously.

**5. continued**

**No:** The oil industry has caused a lot of damage to the rainforest in the Niger Delta by causing some areas to be cleared for pipelines; settlers have used these pathways to gain access to clear more of the forest causing irreversible damage; there have been a very large number of oil leaks causing land to become polluted; and damaging the local fishing; as well as damaging the local environment, the oil industry may be contributing to global climate change/increasing $CO_2$ levels both by destroying the rainforest and allowing more fossil fuels to be burned.

6.   *1 mark per valid point. 2 marks per expanded point.*

Possible answers might include:

Country in debt has to pay large amount of money to its lenders; this means there is less money available to the country; so it cannot invest in new business; which means fewer goods are exported; so the country goes further into debt; it also means there is less money to spend on social services, education or health care.

7.   *1 mark per valid point. 2 marks per extended point.*

Possible answers might include:

Support by guaranteeing minimum price for products of developing countries; middlemen who cream off profits are cut out of process; more of the money goes to the communities; they can then invest this money in new projects and so improve the quality of life; people in developed countries may pay slightly more for such commodities but they know this helps their partners in trade; since a higher proportion of the value of the product goes direct to the farmers; growers protected by guaranteed price from price fluctuation.

8.   (a)   *Techniques selected must be justified in detail.*

Possible answers might include:

Information could be put into rank order; which would allow people to note relative importance of each country's statistics; map could be drawn in proportion to population size with other statistics superimposed as pie or bar graphs; which would allow data to be shown on one source; shaded world map could be drawn; to show source high/low GDP effectively; various scattergraphs could be used; to show clear relationships between sets of data; bar graphs could be used to show imports and exports; pie charts could be drawn to compare, eg population to land area; allows clear comparisons between areas.

# Geography Credit
# Level 2000 (cont.)

**8.** *(b)*     *No marks for choice. 1 mark per valid point. 2 marks per expanded point.* Possible answers might include:

**Yes:** USA has second largest population and is most wealthy; while Brazil with a lower population has much poorer GDP and level of exports/ imports; USA with one of largest land areas has highest levels of exports/imports; India has low land area relative to US and Brazil suggesting it has fewer resources for its population and so has low GDP/head; also it has smaller percent of population in urban areas suggesting it is not economically dominant.

**No:** no clear cut relationship because Brazil has large area but low export/import figures; while India with huge population (882m) has lowest GDP of all; and a very small urban population (25%) which is not typical of dominant countries; Japan is second for trade and second wealthiest yet has the smallest population and land area; Russia despite having largest land area has relatively low imports/exports.

**9.** *1 mark per valid statement. 2 marks per expanded point.*

Possible answers might include:

Most population in pockets along coast which provides fishing opportunities; high population close to mineral deposits due to employment opportunities; valleys have higher population density due to water supply and flat land for building; low population density in some mountain areas due to difficult living conditions.

# Geography Credit
# Level 2001

**1.** *(a)*   (i)    *4 correct—3 marks*
*2 or 3 correct—2 marks*
*1 correct—1 mark*

| | |
|---|---|
| Pyramidal Peak: | 860601 |
| Hanging Valley: | 952588 |
| Arête: | 925576 |
| Corrie: | 923580 |

   (ii)   *1 mark for each valid point. 2 marks for a developed point. Full marks can be obtained by an annotated diagram. Only explanatory points will be credited.*

**1. (a) (ii) continued**

**Hanging Valley:** This feature is the result of glacial erosion. A powerful main glacier cuts out a deep valley; but the glacier in the tributary valley does not erode so deeply. As a result when the ice melts there is a very steep slope where the tributary (hanging) valley meets the main valley.

**Pyramidal Peak:** This feature is the result of glacial erosion; and also frost shattering of a peak protruding above the ice. During ice-age conditions a number of corries are cut into the slopes of the mountain. As time passes they are cut further back into the mountain which eventually takes on the appearance of a pyramid or tower-like structure.

**Corrie:** These are formed in steep sided hollows in north facing sides of mountains. Snow accumulates and gradually turns to ice. Movement of ice causes erosion on both the floor and sides of the hollow. Erosion takes place through "plucking" and "abrasion". The hollow becomes concave and the edge of the hollow becomes ridge-shaped. If the hollow fills up with ice some of the ice moves down the slope to a lower level. When ice melts it leaves a deep "arm chair shaped" hollow on the side of the mountain.

**Arête:** as corrie formation followed by—When two corries form back to back on adjacent sides of a mountain, they will be separated by a steep knife-shaped ridge. When fully formed this ridge is called an arête.

*(b)*   *1 mark for each valid reason.*

More than half of Area B belongs to the National Trust for Scotland.

Area A is more accessible from the main road.

The land in Area A is not as steep as in Area B.

Area B is much higher or colder than Area A.

Soils are likely to be thinner/more cliffs/rock outcrops in Area B.

*(c)*   *1 mark for a basic point. 2 marks for a developed point.*

**Advantages**
Dam at lip of hanging valley; provides deep reservoir. Many streams supply water to the reservoir. Large numbers of streams suggest impermeable underlying rock; so good site for reservoir. Power station will be beside sea where spent water can be discharged. Big difference in height between power station and dam and this is approximately 200 metres. Easy access for construction traffic by the A896.

**1. (c) continued**

**Disadvantages**

Disturbance to people at Annat by construction traffic. Loch Torridon Hotel may have to be demolished; denying locals access to the pub. Woodlands may be destroyed/flooded. The scenery will be spoiled; as a river bed with little water can look ugly. The appearance of the waterfall will be ruined.

(d) *1 mark for each valid point.*
*2 marks for a developed point. Argument of both sides will be accepted. Maximum 1 mark for appropriate grid reference.*

**No**

Large scale tourist development would endanger the beauty and landscape quality of the Torridon area. The local population is small so there is no need for a large scale employer likely to spoil the environment of the area. More tourism to the area is likely to result in more people going into the mountains and getting into dangerous situations; particularly when the weather is bad. The A896 along Glen Torridon is a narrow road and could not cope with increased traffic and making it wider would damage the environment of the glen. A large scale tourist development is likely to conflict with the conservation aims of the National Trust. There is already a Countryside centre (905557) in Torridon. Area is remote/isolated.

**Yes**

A large tourist development in a beautiful mountain area will attract lots of visitors; who will bring in money; and help create employment in the area. A big tourist development will keep young people in the area by providing jobs and social attractions. Loch Torridon and Loch Damh offer great potential for a major water sports development project. A large tourist project is likely to bring more customers to local businesses such as Loch Torridon Hotel (888542). Increased erosion of popular hill paths will be an acceptable price to pay for the economic benefits to the area.

(e) *A maximum of 3 marks may be awarded for detailed description of techniques. A minimum of 2 techniques must be stated.*

**Techniques**

The student can use the photograph to help add extra information and annotations to the sketch. The Geology map can be used to help add geological information to the sketch; and this could be in the form of an overlay.

The student can use the contours on the map to draw a cross-section from the viewpoint to the summit of Beinn Alligin.

**1. (e) continued**

**Justification**

Annotations draw attention to features/relationships of particular relevance/significance.

The overlay technique could show the relationship between the rock types of the area and the relief as shown on the sketch.

The cross-section would show the height and slope of the land along the selected line. Geology/ land use/land cover/settlement could be added to show possible relationships.

2. *1 mark for each relevant point.*
*2 marks for a developed point.*

**No**

The Tourist Board will be concerned that National Park status will mean more planning controls; likely to interfere with tourist related developments/projects. Conservationists will worry that the new status for the area will attract too many tourists; who will put more pressure on the environment of the area. More people coming to the area will mean heavy recreation use of forests and the Forestry Commission will be concerned about fire and possible damage to young trees. Farmers will worry about possible restrictions on how they farm their land within the National Park. Planning permission for house building is likely to become more difficult to get.

**Yes**

Farmers will see the increased number of visitors to the area as an opportunity to diversify; into tourist related projects such as providing accommodation. Farmers are also likely to welcome any grants available for farming in sympathy with the environment of the new National Park. Conservationists will be happy at the prospect of stricter controls on developments, such as building, within the area of the new "park". The Water Board may feel that national park status will make it easier to restrict visitor access in areas where water might get contaminated. Housing developers may think that the new status for the area will attract more people to live in the settlements in and around "the park" so that demand for housing will rise.

3. *1 mark for each relevant explanatory point. 2 marks for an expanded point.*

There is an occluded front; which is likely to bring heavy rain and poor visibility. The isobars are tightly packed and this indicates that winds will be very strong. Winds move anticlockwise round low pressure so the yachts would have to sail into the strong wind. The sea will be rough and the sailors' lives would be in danger.

# Geography Credit
# Level 2001 (cont.)

4.  (a)  *At least 2 of the data sets to be referred to for maximum marks. Where no reasons given mark out of 4.*

    **Building Height**

    Count number of storeys in each building in sample section, so that average height of building can be calculated.

    **Pedestrians**

    Take up position in the middle of the sample section and count the number of pedestrians who pass within a given time. This technique will show the relationship between intensity of land use and number of pedestrians.

    **Land Use**

    Pace out or measure the frontage of buildings recording their use. The total length of each land use along the sample section can then be calculated; from which percentages/pie segment angles can be worked out; to enable the proportion of each land use to be calculated. Interview tenants to find out land use. This provides accurate information on internal land use which may not be visible from outside.

    (b)  *Where answer is pure description, a maximum of 2 marks. Maximum of 1 mark for reference to accessibility in centre of city, but without further explanation such as convergence of "A" class roads, bus/rail stations etc.*

    Building height increases towards the centre due to greater demand for land. The only way to develop is upwards making maximum use of highly expensive land.

    Open space decreases towards the centre because of the increased demand for land.

    The number of pedestrians increases towards the centre because there are many shops there and many people who work in offices.

    Hotels/entertainments/shops/offices/public buildings are located near centre due to accessibility; because "A" class roads meet there; and the rail and bus stations.

    Residential land use decreases towards the centre because land is very expensive; as a result of the high demand from other land users; such as shops and offices. Air quality/noise/traffic congestion/parking problems make living in the centre less desirable.

5.  *1 mark for each valid point.*
    *2 marks for a developed point.*

    A location where the environment is high quality will make it easier to attract highly skilled staff; because families will be willing to move to attractive areas. Nearness to universities is important for research and development and for a supply of graduates from which to choose highly qualified staff. A good transport infrastructure is vital for taking in components and sending out finished products as well as getting workers to the factory. There are advantages if the neighbouring industries can supply materials/components or if they have resulted in the build up of a workforce skilled in working in high technology industry. Government incentives provided through agencies such as Scottish Enterprise have persuaded firms to come to Scotland because they cut the cost of setting up in a new location.

6.  (a)  *1 mark for a relevant point. 2 marks for a developed point. Must mention both north and south for full marks. Must refer to both births **and** infant mortality for full marks.*

    In general the North has fewer births per woman; and a lower infant mortality rate. On average, a woman in the developing world has twice as many children as in the developed world. Infant mortality is eight times higher in developing countries. In Botswana, women have 4·3 babies on average, whereas in Japan they have 1·4.

    (b)  *1 mark for a relevant explanatory point. 2 marks for a developed point. Descriptive points for part (a) if needed will be credited.*

    Developed countries of the North have well established family planning services. Higher infant mortality makes it difficult for many couples in developing countries to accept birth control. Poor diet and very limited medical provision mean higher infant mortality in developing countries. In developed countries there are more opportunities for women to have a career outside the home. This results in them having fewer children.

    (c)  *1 mark for each relevant point. 2 marks for a developed point. Both population growth and infant mortality must be referred to for full marks.*

    Programmes to improve child health and thus reduce infant mortality will encourage couples to have fewer children. Improve education of women so that they will become aware of the importance of clean water and hygiene as well as the advantages of birth control. More education gives women the opportunities for a career and this often persuades them to have fewer children. Provide incentives such as grants of money to families who limit the number of children; or pass laws to penalise couples who have more than one or two babies; as with the one child policy of China.

**7.** (a) *1 mark for a relevant point.*
*2 marks for a developed point.*

By 2050 there will be many more old people in Japan.

By 2050 the birth rate will have fallen and life expectancy will have increased. The pyramid structure of 1950 will have been replaced by a much straighter structure by 2050. In 1950 there were about 30 million people under 15 years.

By 2050 less than 20 million will be in this category. Necessary to mention "change".

(b) *1 mark for a relevant point.*
*2 marks for a developed point.*

**Yes:**

More old people to support. Older people require specialised facilities such as housing; and medical facilities; and the government will have to find money to pay for these. There may be a shortage of skilled young people to staff key industries and services. With all the older people there will be a high dependency ratio.

**No:**

Fewer children so the government will not have to provide so many schools; and spend so much on child medical care. The decline in the number of young people means there is no prospect of runaway population growth. Younger people are likely to have less competition for employment.

**8.** (a) *1 mark for a relevant point.*
*2 marks for a developed point. Maximum of 2 marks for a list.*

Kenya's main exports are raw materials/foodstuffs; while the main imports are manufactured goods. Exports of finished goods make up a small proportion of total. Proportion of minerals and fuels (imports/exports) are roughly similar. Total value of exports is lower than imports by about $1100 million so Kenya has a severe trade deficit. Kenya's main trade partner (both imports and exports) is the European Union. Kenya has considerable exports to other African countries but only 2% imports are from that continent. Japan and the UAE are important suppliers to Kenya.

(b) *Description of techniques and justification required. For full marks at least 2 techniques must be used.*

Export/import figures could be set out in a pair of pie charts; because pie chart segments show relative proportions which are easily compared. Pie charts could be drawn with different radii to emphasize that import total is greater than exports.

Flow lines could be used entering and leaving maps of Kenya. The flow lines can be drawn in a thickness proportional to the percentage of imports/exports showing how important each trading partner is to Kenya.

**8. (b) continued**

Use an overlay on a world map which shows the trading partners of Kenya. For each trading partner the overlay shows a pair of bar graphs illustrating the percentage of Kenya's imports and exports. Placing two graphs together allows easy comparison of relative value of imports/exports; as well as showing the world location of Kenya's trading partners.

# Geography
# Credit Level 2002

1. *Answers worth more than 1 mark are indicated by the marks shown in brackets immediately following the statement.*

2. *A maximum 1 mark will be awarded for appropriate grid reference.*

**1.** (a) Answers may refer to both points of view.

**Yes**: It provides access from W and NW to the industrial estates at Altens and Tullos. It follows a route that is not very built up so that there will be least disturbance to the majority of the population in the Aberdeen area (2). It will speed up travel between S and NW of Aberdeen. It will reduce traffic congestion in the centre of Aberdeen since through traffic will be able to by-pass the city (2). It provides good access to the airport. It starts at an existing interchange on the A90T at 932004. Part of the route is already disfigured by pylons.

**No:** It will use valuable farmland on the edge of the city. It will disturb some settlements such as Milton of Myrtle at 876022 (2). It will be very expensive because it will be 13 km long (2) and a bridge will have to be built over the R Dee at 880014 (2). It breaches the Green Belt and will be unsightly (2). It will have a big impact on the environment since it cuts across forest walks (2).

(b) **Similarities:**

There are modern street patterns at the edge of Aberdeen indicating new housing as shown at the urban fringe of the model. Sheddocksley on 8906 is an example of this. Moving east the housing appears to get older as indicated by the more rectangular pattern in 9106. Further east in 9026 there appears to be an area of older buildings which could be tenements or industries as shown in the model. This merges into the CBD in 9306 as in the model. There is an open space; Green Belt beyond the city.

# Geography
## Credit Level 2002 (cont.)

### 1. (b) continued

**Differences:**

There is no commuter settlement shown on the model but there is at the W edge of the map transect at Kingswells. There are no obvious big factories before you get to the CBD of Aberdeen, but instead, there is a school at 931062 (2). The CBD is not at the E edge of the transect through Aberdeen. There is a zone of docks and industries on the E side of Aberdeen's CBD which is not on the model.

(c) 1  Located beside river because paper mills need water for processing and river would originally have been a source of power (3).

2  Located beside docks where N Sea fishing boats can unload their produce (2). It is also conveniently located on the shore of the N Sea where oil is being extracted—thus Aberdeen is an accessible port for servicing oil vessels (2). Being right beside the sea means there are no transport costs involved in moving the fish to the processing plants.

3  Modern industrial estates are located on the edge of the city where land is cheap and traffic congestion is not a problem (2). They are accessible by road eg Altens Estate is close to a roundabout on the A956 at 946029, allowing easy access for workforce and for distribution of products and bringing in raw materials (2). The industrial estates at Dyce are conveniently situated for the airport to allow easy import of light raw materials and quick transport for management (2).

(d)  Answers should show the link between physical features and land use.

There are very few buildings on the floodplain due to the danger of flooding (2). Instead the land on the floodplain is used for farming or recreation eg golf course in 8802 (2). The fertile alluvial soils on the floodplain will help farming. The line of the valley has been used as a routeway on both sides—on the north of the A93 and in the past a railway and the B9077 on the south (2). All these communications run SW–NE the same line as the valley. The river is a barrier to N–S communications.

The southerly aspect of the N side of the valley provides a pleasant site for the settlements of Cults and Bieldside. The steepest slopes are wooded eg at 876015 and 912029 (2) as is the inaccessible island at 867010 (2). The river provides a source of water for the reservoir at 901027 (2).

1. (e)  Answers may include:
**Advantages:**

The land is flat for building on and there is land to expand on to the N (2). There are good railway links to Aberdeen including a railway station at Dyce and a dual carriageway into the city—the A96(T) (2). The nearby industrial estates will benefit from being able to send and receive freight easily by air. The airport is close to Aberdeen, keeping journey times for passengers down (2). Flights approaching from the N and SW will not have to pass over housing areas.

**Disadvantages:**

Planes approaching from or taking off towards the E and SE will have to pass over dense housing areas, causing noise pollution and safety fears (2). Buildings to the E and W limit possibilities for expansion in these directions.

2.  Created by glacial erosion. As climate cools snow gathers in a hollow on the side of a mountain. As snow accumulates snow becomes compressed into ice. Ice starts to move down hill under gravity. Plucking takes place at the back of the hollow and abrasion on the floor of the hollow (2). Freeze/thaw action widens the joints at the back of the hollow making plucking more effective. A rotary movement of the ice forms a lip to the hollow. When the ice melts a deep armchair shaped hollow is left.

3. (a)  Winds are SW and 15 knots. Temperature is 8 °C, which is mild for winter. Pressure is 1004 mb. There is no rain and cloud cover is 4 oktas.

(b)  Answers must have **explanatory** points eg:

Heavy showers because of advancing cold front. Showers will give way to clearer conditions as the front moves away. Temperatures will fall because of advancing cold front. Sunny intervals since air behind the cold front has mostly clear skies. Lighter winds because isobars further apart.

4.  **Advantages:**

It will be a good place to generate wind power because it is windy on top of a hill and Orkney often gets high winds (2). 25% of Orkney's electricity will come from here. This means the islands will be more self sufficient in power supplies. The wind turbines will not create air pollution.

**Disadvantages:**

Some people might complain that the turbines are an eyesore. There might be some noise pollution for the surrounding area. There will have to be alternative sources of power for spells of calm weather. The birds in the nearby RSPB reserve might be disturbed by the turbines.

5. (a) **Gathering:**

Could interview; give questionnaire to shoppers in a large shopping centre, asking where they have come from (2). Interview/ write letter to/ask manager of a department store or newspaper for a record of their delivery area (2). Ask manager of Caley Thistle FC for the addresses of their season ticket holders; the hospital for addresses of their patients (2).

**Justifications:**

These are high order services which will represent the longest distances that people will be prepared to travel to Inverness to use its services (2). These points can be plotted on a map and the boundary of the sphere of influence can be drawn around them. Using several services allows a combined sphere of influence to be drawn which will be more accurate; realistic.

(b) Answers could include:

It extends a long distance to the N and W because this area is sparsely populated with no other settlements of a comparable size (2). It does not extend far to the E and S because in these directions there are much bigger settlements such as Aberdeen and Glasgow, which will have higher order services to attract people from further away (2). Also there is the barrier of the Grampian mountains which restricts access from the south (2).

6. (a) Fields have been made bigger to make it easier to use machines and to help increase yields (2). Farmworkers' cottages have been sold off because less labour is needed nowadays and the farmer may get extra income by renting some out as holiday cottages (2). New crops are being grown because of changing market demand. Land has been set aside because too much food is being produced and the government EU gives the farmer a grant for this (2). The farmer has introduced some leisure facilities; visitor attractions to get more money.

(b) Likely **techniques**: pie charts, bar graphs; histograms, divided bar graphs, classification

**Justifications:**

**Pie charts:**

A clear way of showing figures given in percentages. A pie chart for each year will allow comparisons to be made easily. Can be enhanced by the use of colour.

**Histograms:**

The differences in land use would be easy to compare in a composite bar graph, where, for 1970 and 2002, a different coloured bar for each land use could be drawn side by side (2) or two separate histograms for each year would allow straightforward comparisons to be made (2).

6. (b) continued

**Divided bar graphs:**

Two separate bar graphs, one above the other, would enable land uses in each year to be compared easily. Land use could be shaded differently for ease of reading.

**Classification:**

Simplifies the data making it easier to process.

7. (a) Possible answers include:

Very few people are found in the mountainous areas because slopes are too steep to build on and the climate too cold and soils too thin for farming (2). The largest population densities are on or close to the best farmland on the drier side of the island (2) where the land is lower and consequently warmer and more suited to agriculture (2). The coal fields are moderately populated because there is employment available.

(b) Answers might include:

A higher proportion of the population of Indonesia is under 15 years of age because birth rates are higher in developing countries, where fewer women get the chance of an education and information on birth control is less easily spread (2). There is a larger share of the New Zealand population in the older age groups because more people have the chance of medical treatment than in a developing country where there is less money to set up enough health centres and hospitals (2). The high living standards in New Zealand mean that there are plenty of opportunities for women to have careers and this reduces the birth rates. Child death rates are higher in developing countries such as Indonesia so people like to have as many children as possible. Religious beliefs and native customs can often make it difficult to persuade people to adopt family planning especially in more remote areas of developing countries (2).

8. *No marks for choice.*
Both points of view can be expressed.

**Agree:**

Developed countries have a larger share of world exports, 80% compared to 20%; four times as much. Developed countries import lots of primary products which will be cheaper to buy. Primary products can be used in developed countries' industries and the manufactured products then exported to earn more money for the country. Developed countries can trade with other developed countries easily especially if they are members of a trading group such as the EU with trade barriers for outsiders (2).

# Geography
# Credit Level 2002 (cont.)

## 8. continued

**Disagree:**

Developing countries do not have a share of world exports. They buy a smaller % of primary and secondary goods so trade is not costing as much as it does for developed countries (2). Developed countries are buying more than ¾ of secondary products which are expensive to buy. Developing countries can trade with developed countries thus earning money from exports.

# Geography
# Credit Level 2003

*Please note:*

- *Points that will gain marks are separated by semicolons (";").*
- *Developed points, appropriate examples and relevant grid references are worth 2 marks. These are noted in the following answer guide with "(2)".*
- *Your answers do not have to include all the points given in the following answer guide. However, to gain high marks, your answers must include enough points to cover the number of marks available for each question.*

1.  (a) (i)  *Four correct:*      *3 marks*
            *Three/two correct:*      *2 marks*
            *One correct:*      *1 mark*

            Hanging valley:      134996
            Truncated spur:      146980
            Corrie:      094992
            U-shaped valley:      155993

       (ii)  eg **Hanging valley**: The result of glacial erosion; Deep steep-sided valley cut by powerful glacier; Processes of abrasion and plucking; Tributary valley not eroded so deeply as occupied by a less powerful glacier; When ice melts the tributary valley drops very steeply down to the floor of the main valley; The mouth of the tributary valley appears to "hang" above the steep side of the main valley.

            eg **Truncated spur**: The result of glacial erosion along a pre-glacial valley; Before the ice age the valley had been less straight and the river had meandered around spurs; The glacier straightened the valley by eroding away the spurs; In places large masses of solid rock were plucked and abraded by the ice to leave steep slabs of rock as cliffs on the valley side.

            Or any other relevant explanatory points.

     (b) *For full marks, your answer must refer to map evidence. Up to 2 marks are available for reference to conflicts in landscape.* Your answer might include the following:

## 1. (b) continued

**Advantages**: areas of remote wildscape and high mountainous scenery normal in National Parks; good road access via A93; Braemar provides 'honeypot' settlement to help protect rest of landscape; variety of animal habitats due to varied river/forest/glaciated scenery; plenty of scenic views (143905) for passive visitors (2); lots of activities, eg mountain climbing, challenging walks, woodland walks for more active visitors.

**Disadvantages:** National park likely to attract more visitors so put more pressure on fragile landscape; area poorly served by roads – only A93 plus two minor roads; so locals and tourists are likely to be inconvenienced by traffic jams; lot of commercial forest areas which detract from natural beauty of scenery; lack of accommodation for large number of visitors; area likely to have cold, wet and cloudy weather which is unlikely to attract visitors.

     (c) Answers must bring out points of difference: eg The River Dee is a much wider river than the Allt an t-Slugain; being over 50 metres wide; The floor of the Dee valley is wide and flat while the Slugain has a more V-shaped valley (2); A large area of the floodplain of the River Dee is marshy land; The Slugain has a steeper gradient than the Dee; and is likely to be faster flowing; An embankment or levee closely follows the north bank of the River Dee; The Dee flows east while the Slugain flows south east; The Dee flows against steep slopes on the south side of the valley but the land slopes very steeply to the Slugain on both sides of the stream.

        Or any other relevant points.

     (d) Answers should be explanatory eg Braemar is the main cluster of population in the map area and has grown up in an accessible location; where the valley of a large tributary meets the Dee; The A93 links Braemar to the south and east; while a minor road follows the Dee west to Invereye; Small hamlet-like clusters and single settlements are found along Dee valley, and the tributary which flows from the south, because of roads; and the availability of flat land; However, these settlements tend to avoid the lowest land of the valley floors because of flood danger; Away from the rivers steep slopes rule out settlement over much of the area; Small settlements have developed along roads/tracks leading to/past Invercauld House (175925) where jobs are likely to be available (2).

        Or any other relevant points.

     (e) Explanatory answers are required; eg The area north of northings 94 is dominated by deer stalking and grouse shooting because it is high and steep; and suitable for few other land uses; Carn Liath in square 1697 reaches

## 1. (c) continued

over 800 metres above sea level and this area will be cold and exposed; The grouse shooting is on slightly lower ground than the main stalking land because there is more shelter for the birds; There are large areas of coniferous forest on the lower hillsides to the north of the Dee because access will be easier; on the less steep slopes; The floodplain of the Dee provides the main area of flat land and this is more sheltered and suitable for grazing and growing some crops (2); Soil is likely to be better here; Because this is near Invercauld House an area of this land is given over to ornamental parkland; The course of the A93 has to follow a narrow strip between flood danger from the river and a very steep slope; The steep slope limits land use to some mixed woodland; Recreation land is found near the summit of Creag Choinnich because it is close to Braemar; and popular with walkers because of the fine views; Sheltered land round a small loch in Corrie Feragie is used for coniferous woodland; Sheep grazing and deer stalking are the main land uses on the higher land further south where slopes are steep/soils poor/weather difficult.

Or any other relevant points.

2. Station: X

**Explanation**: eg Summer anticyclones bring high temperatures and very little cloud as shown at X (2); Anticyclones usually have light winds as shown by the widely spaced isobars; The light winds blow clockwise round anticyclones and this gives a SW wind at Edinburgh.

*Marks can also be given for reasons against choosing Y or Z.*

eg 5 degrees Celsius at Y is too cold for a summer anticyclone; Z has almost total cloud cover and also some rain and is more typical of depression weather conditions (2).

3. eg Desert expanding south because less rain now falling (drought); Wind from north picks up sand and blows it south; Waterholes dry up because less water in the region; and animals have used up the water; Increased irrigation has caused water levels to fall; Farmers cutting down more bush to grow crops; causing loss of protective tree cover resulting in soil erosion; Animals overgrazing the land since they have lost a lot of older grazing land; Trees are cut down to provide farmland as population increases; more trees are also needed for firewood, therefore soil is exposed to weathering/erosion; Population increase puts pressure on the land.

Or any other relevant points.

4. eg A good defensive position; within a meander; Castle is able to guard the narrow neck of the meander; Early growth was restricted by the meander; and bridges had to be built to enable the town to expand.

## 4. continued

Danger of flooding on floodplain has limited settlement; and land use on the flood plain has been limited to activities not permanently damaged by flooding; These include sports/recreation grounds, parks, agricultural showground.

Or any other relevant points.

5. Answers should be explanatory:

**Physical**: eg Much of the farm is mountainous and the steep slopes are only suitable for rough grazing for sheep; The wet and cloudy climate likely to be found in a mountainous area makes the farm unsuitable for large-scale cultivation of cereals; Much of the lower land is given over to grass which grows well in the damp climate; Grazing is a better use of land than crop growing because soils are thin and infertile over most of the farm; Crop growing does not take place on the low flat land close to the river because of drainage and flood problems; An area close to the farmhouse is used for barley and root crops because it is flat land and easier to cultivate; and above the flood danger level.

**Human**: eg The farmer grows some crops such as barley, turnips, and grass for silage, in order to provide winter feed for animals; The farmer grows trees on some of his steeper land because grants are available for this; and the trees also help to provide shelter for livestock; The land use carried out on this farm depends heavily on grants/subsidies/price support from the Government and EU; The farmer sticks with the land uses shown because his land is likely to be a considerable distance from major centres of population and this limits his scope for diversification projects (2).

Or any other relevant points.

6. Plenty flat land to build on as well as room for expansion (2); There are storage areas for new vehicles around the site; and plenty of room for workers to park their cars; There is a big workforce close by in Newcastle and Sunderland; where redundancies in engineering industries mean that many skilled workers will be looking for employment; There may have been government grants for locating in an area of high unemployment; The site is very accessible for lorries being close to several "A" class roads and the M1 motorway (2); Washington is close to the port of Newcastle and Sunderland, allowing components to be shipped in or vehicles to be exported by sea (2).

Or any other relevant points.

7. (a) *You must refer to both economies and environments for full marks*

eg Disused canals will have been cleaned up and landscaped; which will help to improve the look of the surrounding area; Many tourists will be attracted to see the Falkirk wheel; and this will bring money to the area; The tourists will go to the visitor centre, buy souvenirs, spend

# Geography
# Credit Level 2003 (cont.)

## 7. (a) continued

money in local shops, and stay in hotels nearby (2); New jobs will be created in the visitor centre for locals; and there will be jobs for construction workers; Wildlife will benefit from the creation of SSSIs along the route; Local tourism will be boosted by people who want to travel along the canal by boat; or who walk/cycle along the towpath away from cars.
Or any other relevant points.

(b) Possible **techniques**: Questionnaire given to local communities/businesses/tourist offices etc; Photographs of areas along the route; Counts of walkers/cyclists/boats along sections of the route – or any other reasonable technique. Answers should not repeat the same justification.

**Justifications**:
**Questionnaire**: Student could find out from the tourist offices if tourist numbers had changed following the opening of the Millenium link; They could ask local hotels whether the number of guests had increased; Businesses close to the canal could be asked whether they had noticed an increase in customer numbers.
**Photographs**: Photos could be taken along sections of the route and compared with old photos to see how the environment had changed; The photos could be taken at regular intervals during and after construction to show development over time.
**Counts**: Surveys of number of boats/walkers/cyclists etc would show whether or not the Millenium link is popular; Surveys done at regular intervals over several months might show whether the project increases in popularity as a tourist attraction or is just a "flash in the pan"; The seasonal impact of the project could also be assessed.

## 8.

(a) eg A significant percentage of the population in Developing countries are illiterate and getting people to read instructions and fill in forms would not be a realistic way of collecting information; Large numbers of people do not speak the official language of the country and having to gather information through a wide variety of tribal languages is difficult; Where the land area is large many parts are likely to be inaccessible with the result that many groups of people are likely to be missed in the census (2); Difficult to reach people in some mountain and forest areas; Good roads are absent from extensive areas of a Developing country; Migrant workers make counting difficult and a characteristic of Developing countries is heavy rural to urban migration and this also makes recording difficult (2); Political divisions within a country can make taking a census dangerous for the enumerators.
Or other relevant points.

8. (b) Population census data will provide the government with information they need to plan improvements in education; and health provision; Data will also help them identify areas of the country where the population is growing, declining or relatively static (2); Information on population change can be used to decide where to target development programmes; and to help prioritise where to spend scarce government money; Where a detailed census can be taken information such as the location and significance of minority tribal and language groups can be obtained (2); Information on population may also be used to attract overseas aid for eg population control; or food production programmes.
Or other relevant points.

## 9. Possible **techniques**:

eg    Rearrange in rank order
       Draw a series of pie charts
       Draw a series of divided bar graphs
       Scatter graph
       Bar graph
Answers should not repeat the same justification.

**Justifications**:
Makes it easy to compare the relative importance of each mineral in terms of reserves and production; Positions could be emphasised by drawing a line to link position of mineral in one order column to its position in the other.

**Pie chart**: Two pie charts for each mineral would enable the world significance of South Africa for each mineral to be accurately shown in percentage terms; Actual percentage can be easily re-calculated by use of a protractor to measure segment angle; Colour can be used to improve the visual impact of the size of the South African segments in relation to the rest of the world.

**Bar graph**; allow visual comparison; bars could be coloured to highlight differences.

**Bar chart**: Horizontal bar charts with columns divided on a percentage basis between South Africa and the rest of the world enable differences to be clearly seen and comparisons to be made (2); Colours can be used to enhance the visual communication.

**Scatter graph**: Could be drawn to help test the idea that percentage of reserves is going to be accurately matched by percentage of production; Residuals/ exceptions to any trend can be easily identified and subjected to further study to try to determine why they are residuals/exceptions (2); Scatter graphs are excellent for bringing out apparent relationships/links.

Or any other relevant points.